The Proceedings of GREAT Day

2015

SUNY Geneseo
Geneseo, NY

About GREAT Day and
The Proceedings of GREAT Day

Geneseo Recognizing Excellence, Achievement & Talent is a college-wide symposium celebrating the creative and scholarly endeavors of our students. In addition to recognizing the achievements of our students, the purpose of GREAT Day is to help foster academic excellence, encourage professional development, and build connections within the community.

Established in 2009, *The Proceedings of GREAT Day* journal compiles and publishes promising student work presented at SUNY Geneseo's GREAT Day symposium. The projects, presentations and research included here represent the academic rigor, multidisciplinary study, and unique creativity of the students taking part in the SUNY Geneseo GREAT Day symposium.

Editors: Carolina D. Fernandez, Geneseo Class of 2016

Brendan Mahoney, Geneseo Class of 2018

Publishing Supervisor: Daniel Ross, Academic Excellence Librarian, Milne Library

Editorial Consultant: Sheryl Larson-Rhodes, Reference & Instruction Librarian, Milne Library

Production Manager: Allison Brown, Digital Publishing Services Manager, Milne Library

Publisher: Milne Library, SUNY Geneseo

These proceedings can be accessed online at greatjournal.geneseo.edu

Acknowledgments

SPECIAL THANKS TO:

Angela Galvan, Digital Resources & Systems Librarian

Patty Hamilton-Rodgers, GREAT Day Coordinator

Katherine Pitcher, Interim Library Director

Leah Root, Publishing & Web Services Developer

Brandon West, Reference & Instruction Librarian

GREAT Day is funded by the Office of the Provost,
the Student Association, Campus Auxiliary Services
and the Jack '76 and Carol '76 Kramer Endowed Lectureship.

The GREAT Day Website: http://www.geneseo.edu/great_day

Table of Contents

An Interview with President Denise Battles

Proceedings of GREAT Day: When did you first attend GREAT Day? What was your favorite thing about it?

President Battles: My first attendance at GREAT Day was last year after I had been identified as incoming president but had not actually started. I arranged a couple of occasions to come to the College in advance of my first day on the job which was July 1, 2015, and I made sure to be here for GREAT Day because I had heard so many wonderful things about it. I am a big believer in students working under the mentorship of faculty and staff to engage in research, scholarship, creative activity, and otherwise explore their academic interests in close collaboration with individuals who have expertise in those areas. I came last April, and I absolutely enjoyed every moment. I had the opportunity to say a few words at one of the events associated with GREAT Day, and I am very much looking forward to this year.

Were you able to observe student work and projects?

Yes. Last year I had the opportunity to sit in on some of the oral presentations. I also participated in the poster session and attended the keynote presentation. So I had a good taste of all the aspects of the day.

How did it feel to see the work students were doing on campus? What kinds of research did you do as an undergraduate?

It was very affirming to see the students applying their studies. By affirming I mean that my impressions about the college were accurate. We have very high caliber students who are performing at a very high level; they are very active, intelligent, and inquisitive. I thought that was the case, but I saw it very well evidenced through my participation in GREAT Day. One of the reasons I found and find the College so appealing is because of the dedication of the faculty and staff and the customized approach they take to assuring that students have every opportunity to explore their academic interests. Being able to witness that process in action very much affirmed that my perceptions were accurate in that regard.

As a student, I was involved in undergraduate research. I went to an institution similar to Geneseo. It was smaller-sized; liberal arts and science were a key focus. As a geology major, I had the opportunity to do undergraduate research under the mentorship of a new faculty member at my institution. Her guidance very impactful for me. She was a high-temperature geochemist in the field of geology. It is probably not a coincidence that I went on to be a high temperature geochemist. I really appreciated the opportunity to learn from her, to work with her.

I was given the opportunity to learn how to utilize a variety of high-tech geochemical instrumentation and was trained and educated on how to use very expensive analytical tools that I do not think I would have had access to in a graduate or research-focused institution. I had experiences that I might not have had in other settings and that helped shaped my desire to pursue my graduate education in geology and ultimately become a faculty member.

Would you say that GREAT Day is an essential part of the Geneseo community?

I think GREAT Day is a truly important aspect of what we do at Geneseo. It encapsulates a lot of what is best about the College in one very rich and full day when you get to see students demonstrate their knowledge and creative abilities, their scholarly work, their research. I think that in the past ten years—because we are about to celebrate our tenth consecutive GREAT Day—GREAT Day has become a strong tradition for Geneseo, and I am delighted that it is an activity that students, faculty, and staff embrace. From year to year, the number of presentations and students participating has steadily risen which indicates just how attractive and appealing the event has become.

Have you seen a similar undergraduate research symposiums at prior universities? What has been your experience with those?

I have seen similar events that focused on undergraduate research, but the fact that Geneseo dedicates a full day to focus on research, scholarly and creative activity makes it different from the settings I have been in before. Elsewhere, such events are an element, an add-on evening kind of thing; that we provide members of the campus community the opportunity to present *and* to attend is something that is distinctive compared to the settings I have been in.

How do you think GREAT Day helps Geneseo as an academic institution? Why is it important?

I think from a student perspective it can be a unique capstone kind of experience. It is one thing to engage in the research, scholarly work, or creative activity under the mentorship of an expert in the field; it's another thing to pull that all together in a professional setting to deliver a performance, a talk, or a poster. It allows students to pull together all of their educational experiences to work on a problem and present it to individuals in a way that actively engages the observer. It enables the student participants to field questions and provide answers from GREAT Day visitors and to perhaps think about the work that they have done in new and different ways.

What do you like to do on your spare time?

I am a geologist, so I like being outdoors and hiking and touring national parks. I love reading; *laughter* I wish I had a little bit more time to engage in that. I have a dog, Texas Lucy, who fortunately likes to go for her paces, so my husband and I regularly have the opportunity to get outside; if only to exercise our pooch.

An Interview with Wendy-Marie Aylward

Hometown: *Olney, MD*

Major: *English with Adolescent Certification*

Hobbies/Inspiration: *Sign language and deaf culture. I am co–president of Gestures: Organization for Deaf Awareness. I like to read a lot. I like to be in dance performances.*

Do/did you like Geneseo? Why did you choose to come to Geneseo?

Wendy: Initially, I came to Geneseo because of the Creative Writing program but I ended up not doing that. I stayed because I really enjoy the atmosphere on campus. The campus just feels very comfortable. Most of the professors are very personable, I feel that I can actually speak with them and inquire for help. There are a lot of opportunities on campus that I probably would not be able to have on a bigger campus because it is easy to get lost in the crowd. I just found a lot of things to do here.

Why do you feel that GREAT Day is important?

Well, there are two main reasons. The first is that GREAT Day is important to students on a personal level. It serves as a great validation and motivation for students to do well, aside from just getting graded, because students have the opportunity to present their own work and the chance to really excel at something. They get to share that with other people. The second reason is that it is good for students to see what their peers are doing. There are all kinds of interesting things that happen in our classes that we lose sight of with all the grading and GPAs and whatnot. We are turning out interesting work that is worth sharing, GREAT Day allows us to see that.

How did it feel to present your work at GREAT Day?

It was nerve-wracking.

Was it different from presenting in a regular classroom?

It definitely was different. I knew that my professor had nominated me, so in a way I felt that I was representing my professor and I did not want to let her down. But, also, people were giving their time to be there and to see my presentation so it was definitely different from a regular class presentation.

Lives and Lies

Wendy-Marie Aylward

Most children are taught from the moment they begin speaking that lying is bad and that if somebody asks a question, the answer should be the truth. But it has long since been recognized that "truth" and "lie" cannot be easily defined as absolutes, and that most matters fall somewhere in between. Meena Kumar from Meera Syal's *Anita and Me* has mastered this grey area, shaping the truth to suit her needs. In this novel, a lie isn't simply a young girl denying that she stole from her mother's purse; it is the twisting of reality, self-deception, and the telling and imagining of half-truths that warp Meena's view of the world. Meena, who is caught between the shame of an Indian heritage and the desire to be truly British, seeks to change the life she has through these deceptions. Her journey towards self-acceptance is reflected in the changing nature of her lies, as she ultimately arrives at a different truth about her friends and her Indian heritage.

Meena deceives herself through the idealization of others' lives, perceiving them as filled with excitement and failing to recognize the sorrow they feel. When Meena sees the "gippos," as Anita's mother calls them, she is fascinated by their lifestyle, imagining "how romantic it must be to just climb in and move off once boredom or routine set in" (Syal, 1997, p. 102). She doesn't realize the implications of what she sees—the "pin-thin children," the "tired, washed-out woman… inhaling deeply on a cigarette," which reveal a life of struggle and strife (Syal, 1997, p. 102). Similarly, she reacts to her family's reminiscence of the past with oblivious insensitivity. When Meena remembers her mother's rickshaw story of a man being stabbed in the face, she is affected only by the "meeting of two worlds, the collision of the epic with the banal" (Syal, 1997, p. 36). Whilst her father grapples with the thought that he might be responsible for someone's death, Meena sighs along only at the thought that her father had planted a "real live bomb" (Syal, 1997, p. 76). One might believe that Meena is truly disturbed for a moment by her family's history as she hides in the darkened stairwell eavesdropping on her Aunties' and Uncles' stories from a violent past. Hearing those stories she feels her "heart…trying to break out of [her] chest," and her sleep that night is "full of blood red trains screaming through empty stations, scattering severed limbs as it whistled past" (Syal, 1997, pp. 74-75). Meena comes to realize that the past she has listened to is a "murky bottomless pool full of monsters…with a deceptively still surface and a deadly undercurrent" (Syal, 1997, p. 75). Yet she is not touched by the horror of the stories she hears, but rather by the thought of their existence, and is terrified that "I would be discovered and they would clam up and deny me more" (Syal, 1997, p. 74). In the end, her concern is not with the pain that her family has felt but with her own ability to cope with the enormity of what she has heard. Most astonishing is her reaction to meeting Mr. Worrall, a man essentially erased and reduced to a motionless moaning figure as a result of the violence of war, who functions as real evidence of what comes from Meena's desired "epic" life. "Now I [know] two war veterans" is the first thing she thinks, followed by a feeling of annoyance that her papa "had not done anything as remotely exciting or dangerous in his youth" (Syal, 1997, p. 66). Thus she sees only the possibilities, the beauty, the adventure, and the glamor in these imagined realities, blind to the sorrow that pervades many of the stories that enthrall her.

Meena takes this idealization of others' lives one step further into the realm of fantasy and complete fabrication, imagining a dramatized "other life" that she cannot see and will never experience for herself. Her own parents' lives are a source of inspiration for young Meena, their past almost like a myth that has lost its magic. She fantasizes about what her life could have been if her father had gone into film and becomes "obsessed with what [she] had missed out on, being the daughter of a famous film hero" (Syal, 1997, p. 82). Meena pictures her mama "singing the song to the wind as she cycled back from her all-girls college…duty and desire already at war for her future" (Syal, 1997, p. 111). Even her loud and plump Auntie

Shaila becomes "pencil-thin in her chic chiffon suit" as she saunters through one of the largest commercial centers in New Delhi, "pretending not to notice, but knowing for certain, that every eye was upon her" (Syal, 1997, p. 111). At times Meena becomes bitter with jealousy about these imagined other lives, as with Anita Rutter's plans to live in a London flat with Sherrie. She conjures an extravagant and impossible image of the two looking out of their penthouse to see "Buckingham Palace, the Tower of London, the Houses of Parliament and several theatres" all in one view (Syal, 1997, p. 99). Meena completely ignores reality, conveniently rearranging the world to suit her desires. I believe it is an overpowering sense of yearning for an unattainable identity that leads Meena to lie and embellish upon the details of her life.

Meena draws inspiration from the thought of being someone else, leading her to create a persona for herself fashioned after the individual whom she finds most exciting and intriguing—Anita Rutter. Meena believes Anita is a girl whose father has been in the Navy and who dares talk back to an adults, and this makes her the perfect combination of adventure and shameless audacity for Meena to emulate. She seems unreal and unreachable, at one point compared to the Cheshire Cat of *Alice in Wonderland*, an often sarcastic character with a disregard for rules and a brazen, decisive way of speaking. Meena looks to Anita to tell her which path she ought to take, just as Alice looks for guidance from the Cheshire Cat. Such an allusion to *Alice in Wonderland* may also imply that Meena, like Alice, is a young girl who does not care which way she goes or who she becomes, so long as she ends up someone very different from who she is now. So Meena chooses the path towards becoming Anita, "the 'cock' of the yard," (Syal, 1997, pp. 38-39) far removed from the "pleasant, helpful, delicate" little Indian girl she is expected to be (Syal, 1997, p. 149). Anita's flair for the dramatic is what draws Meena to her, and she pounces on the first chance she has to link herself to Anita. Upon the discovery of Mrs. Christmas's death, Meena immediately concludes and she and Anita are "murderers…joined in sin," effectively connecting the two (Syal, 1997, p. 78).

With this, Meena embarks on a journey to transform herself into Anita through imitation. Each time she pretends to know what Anita knows, such as what a virgin is, or what it means to want to "shag the arse" off of something, she creates an image of herself that is more like Anita. She wears the mask of Anita when she applies her mother's lipstick, a "glaring cerise grin…seemingly hovering above [her face] like the Cheshire Cat smile," (Syal, 1997, p. 107) the same "Cheshire Cat's smile" she later goes chasing after, as Anita disappears into the grounds of the Big House (Syal, 1997, p. 124). One might suggest that Meena is wearing her mother's make-up and therefore imitating her mother, not Anita. However, I think it is far more significant that Meena ventures to try on her mother's makeup after hearing Anita complain about how she couldn't get into her own mother's stash of makeup, as well as watching Anita and her friends fuss over their faces of eye-shadow, blush, and lip gloss. Soon, Anita and Meena become "officially 'mates,'" (Syal, 1997, p. 135) strolling around together every day, "always aware that we were simply too big and beautiful for Tollington" (Syal, 1997, p. 134). At this point Meena takes on that role of "posturing and looking mean" just as she has seen Anita do countless times before, knowing that she looks the part of a tough Tollington wench as opposed to a sweet Indian girl (Syal, 1997, p. 136). However, it is still a façade, as she remains in awe of Anita and is only projecting an image of her desired self. It is when Meena turns on her own family and cuts those ties that she completes the transformation and becomes the "Anita" she has always wanted to be.

The pinnacle of this transformation, when she effectively realizes her ideal persona and gains Anita's acceptance, is Meena's shameless manipulation of her "cousins," Pinky and Baby. Meena's attitude from the moment she is left alone with her cousins shifts instantly into the standard disdain required of her new identity, and while she does intimidate them into silence, she isn't entirely malicious either. However, this quickly changes when Meena decides to steal the charity money in Mr. Ormerod's shop, as she directly threatens Baby with, "Yow say anything, and yow'm dead" (Syal, 1997, p. 155). Though this is not the first time she steals, as she has stolen from her parents many times before, it is the first time she bullies another person into doing what she wants them to do in order to achieve her goal. She has seen Anita exert the same power over Sherrie and Fat Sallie—playing one girl against the other to compete for her favor—

as well as the members of the "Wenches Brigade," especially against Tracy during the pissing competition when she pushes her weaker younger sister into pulling down her trousers (Syal, 1997, p. 138). It is this same ruthless coercion that Meena turns on Baby and Pinky, manipulating them into remaining silent about the theft even long after it happens. It is then, when Anita softly tells Meena, "You'm a real Wench," when Meena gains Anita's approval and recognition of Meena as her "joint leader," when she finally earns her Wench Wings "without even trying," that Meena's transformation is complete (Syal, 1997, p. 156). Not only has she turned against her own family and proven herself as Anita's equal, but she also feels no guilt over her actions (Syal, 1997). She claims that she does not know she has broken free of, but I think that at that moment what she breaks free of is the mold of her old life, the "Meena beti" she was before. She feels free and unfettered and unbelievably thrilled.

Yet if this fulfillment is what truly brings her happiness, this "breaking free" of an old identity to effectively become an entirely new person, why doesn't the novel end there? I would suggest that this is because *Anita and Me* is an exemplary *bildungsroman*, which, according to Berthold Schoene-Harwood (1999), "insist[s] on the narrative consistency of their characters, suggesting that, whilst they grow and evolve, they do not in fact change, but remain essentially identical with whom they were at the outset and will be in conclusion" (p. 1). For the first part of this novel, Meena devotes her energies to becoming someone different from her family and their expectations. Yet once she achieves her dream of becoming a true Tollington Wench, accepted by her British peers, she begins to defend the part of herself which she previously rejected. I wouldn't argue that Meena, after all her experiences, does not grow and change in any way, however; she comes to accept all parts of herself and embraces the identity she had from the moment she was born, which, "for the first time ever, fitted me to perfection and was all mine" (Syal, 1997, p. 326). This process is supported by Maria Lima (1993), who asserts that "post-colonial writers have used the bildungsroman as a way … to explore precisely the complexities and contradictions of growing up in a region where (post)colonial and racial relationships" are at play (p. 440). At 10 years old, Meena is the

person she's yearned to be for many years, but she is still not happy with who she is, the Black British girl with an Indian heritage. She does, however, come to love herself and her family as she has never done before, and this second transformation into a confident "Meena" who is happy to be herself is reflected in the changing nature of her lies.

Up until this point, Meena's lies have been largely in pursuit of creating a new persona for herself, but once she achieves that goal, they change to a method of defense for herself and her family. When Mr. Ormerod comes to her home to reclaim the tin charity box, she uses a lie to protect herself from the wrath of her father, unthinkingly blaming the theft on Baby. Once again, this is not the first time Meena lies, but as with Meena's previous thefts, nobody had been hurt because of her stubborn lies and fanciful thinking. This is the first time Meena deviates from the lies she uses to change herself since she begins imitating Anita's persona. It is a selfish lie—one told with the intention of covering up her crime regardless of the innocents who might suffer because of it—but it is a lie of defense. However, as Meena begins to grow and learn to empathize with other individuals, her deceptions begin to come to the defense of, quite significantly, the members of her family. Meena struggles with facing judgment and prejudice towards her Indian heritage throughout her life, such as in school when they "do" India. So when she sees Anita judging her parents at their own dinner table, she leaps to their defense with a blatant lie, determined not to let Anita "play the same games with my parents that had made me dizzy and confused" (Syal, 1997, p. 255).

Meena not only uses lies to protect her parents from other people's judgment but also uses them to lessen the burden she places upon her family. She could have told her parents the truth about how and why she broke her leg from riding Trixie, yet she only tells them that she had "fallen awkwardly," minimizing the event rather than milking it for all it's worth and using the event to add excitement to her life as she would have before (Syal, 1997, p. 284). She later reflects, "I was a grown-up now, I had seen my parents swallow down anger and grief a million times, for our sakes" (Syal, 1997, p. 288). She returns this favor when she pretends not to be upset by her Nanima's departure, upon which she reflects, "It was not so hard to do, this sacrificial lark" (Syal, 1997, p. 288). She pretends like this once before—before she becomes best mates with Anita—when, reeling with the hatred expressed against her, she decides not to tell her papa about the old lady who calls her a "bloody stupid wog" once she sees on her father's face the countless times he had protected her from that same truth (Syal, 1997, p. 97). This, in my opinion, is in following with the generic conventions of the bildungsroman, reinforcing the idea that Meena at the end of the novel is essentially the same person she is at the beginning; she only needs to go through struggle and change to learn to be happy with herself and her life.

With the realization of her desired persona, Meena comes to see herself and others from a realistic perspective, and finally learns that she does not need to live a lie to be happy. Finally at the top of the hierarchy alongside Anita, where she thought she'd be happier, Meena comes to see the people she once feared and adored as they really are. Deirdre, whose expression of "dark, knowing hunger" (Syal, 1997, p. 55) always terrified Meena, loses her menace when Meena recognizes "something unexpected in her face—she was frightened of us" (Syal, 1997, p. 215). No longer fighting to become Anita's equal, she is able to see some of the power she and her family possess in their own right, like a million brightly shining stars clear in the night sky without the light of the sun to drown them out. Similarly, she loses her awe and devotion to Anita once she is able to see her on equal ground, realizing that Anita is no more than a girl herself whose own wishful thinking prevents her from seeing through her mother's false promises. Meena even takes it one step further when she entertains the thought that it is Anita who needs her, stepping over the "fine line between love and pity" to completely reverse their roles in her mind (Syal, 1997, p. 242). Meena is finally able to see the hollow and contrived nature of her past fantasies when she strips "Sam the Hero" of his glory to reveal "Sam the Drunk…Sam the Idiot…Sam the…" (Syal, 1997, p. 311). She cannot bring herself to think that Sam's cavalier treatment of girls could indicate something far worse. Beyond letting go of her old, elaborately crafted illusions, Meena also learns that the "drama and excitement" she has prayed for so fervently are linked to real pain and sorrow, and that "change always strolled hand in hand with loss" (Syal, 1997, p. 197). In that new state of thinking it is unlikely that she will still yearn to hear more of her Aunties' and Uncles' stories of Partition as she did hiding in the darkened stairwell a lifetime ago.

The coming of Meena's Nanima, along with Meena's disillusionment, is key to helping Meena come to terms with her own situation in life. Before Nanima, all the stories Meena had heard were abstract and distant; seeing her grandmother in the flesh serves to solidify those accounts of India and give them personal shape and substance. Nanima's own stories take on more weight when one considers that all the other stories Meena had heard were treated as taboo by her mother, given as a precious "gift" by her father, or secretly stolen from her Aunties and Uncles; Nanima instead chooses to recall her experiences in India unabashedly in loud Punjabi, not as story but as fact. "They all put mama's rickshaw story and papa's unexploded bomb into kind of context for me," Meena reflects, as she realizes from hearing Nanima's anecdotes that she is not witnessing a grand adventure, but simply life as it was—as regular as falling off a horse or ending up in a hospital (Syal, 1997, p. 211). In the end, she comes to accept the truth as "enough excitement for a lifetime already" (Syal, 1997, p. 303).

Witnessing Nanima's loud and unabashed ownership of India's history also pushes Meena to realize her own previous feeling of shame about her heritage when she "did" India in school, specifically the Black Hole of Calcutta. The "Black Hole of Calcutta" refers to an event in India where Indian troops captured a post held by the Dutch East India Trading Company. A captured soldier by the name of Holwell (1764) described it as "a hundred and forty-six wretches… crammed together in a cube of about eighteen feet, in a close sultry night, in Bengal" (p. 258). This version of the story, according to Bruce Heydt (2003), "enjoyed widespread acceptance" for more than 150 years (p. 15). It wasn't until 1959, less than a decade before the time the novel takes place, that author Brijen Gupta revealed that the number of people captured was "about 64 and the number of survivors was 21," (Heydt, 2003, p. 15) as opposed to the originally reported 146 people with 23 survivors. This kind of history, paired with images of "angry unruly mobs, howling like animals for the blood of the brave besieged British" found in Meena's textbooks, weighs down on Meena for most of her life, driving her to reinvent herself (Syal, 1997, p. 211). Now, with Nanima, she is able to let go of that shame, and feel how "for the first time [she] desperately wanted to visit India and claim some of [that] magic" (Syal, 1997, p. 211). As Meena comes to love and accept her Indian heritage, she no longer needs the crutch of lies and fabrication to create a desired alternate persona. She is able to find satisfaction in her own identity.

Meena Kumar presents a complex character who transitions from envying the lives and fabricated lies of other people, to finding contentment and even joy in her own life and identity. She recalls how as a very young child she nearly chokes on a hot dog in the back of her parents' car, basking in the thrill of the occasion while imagining the screaming headline, "TOT CHOKES ON UNCOOKED SAUSAGE," announcing her death (Syal, 1997, p. 37). Yet she does not resent Tracy in the least for what Meena once thought of a dramatic experience, nor the ironically similar headline "Tot Comes Back From the Dead" celebrating Tracy's miraculous recovery (Syal, 1997, p. 321). She does not need to envy anyone else's life anymore. By the end of the novel Meena has transformed herself into Anita and back again, gradually shedding the need to rely upon lies to improve her existence, till at last she is able to move on with her life—her own life and nobody else's.

REFERENCES

Black Hole of Calcutta. (2016). In *Encyclopædia Britannica*. Retrieved from http://www.britannica.com/topic/Black-Hole-of-Calcutta

Carroll, L. & Gardner, M. (1960). *The Annotated Alice: Alice's Adventures in Wonderland & Through the Looking Glass*. New York, NY: C.N. Potter.

Heydt, B. (2003). Just how 'black' was it? *British Heritage, 24*(4) 14-16.

Holwell, J. Z., et al. (1764). *India Tracts*. London, England: T. Becket and P. A. de Hondt. Retrieved from http://catalog.hathitrust.org/Record/002240163

Lima, M. H. (1993). Decolonizing genre: Jamaica Kincaid and the bildungsroman. *Genre: Forms of Discourse and Culture, 26*(4), 431-459.

Schoene-Harwood, B. (1999). Beyond (t)race: Bildung and proprioception in Meera Syal's Anita and Me. *The Journal of Commonwealth Literature, 34*(1), 159-168. doi:10.1177/002198949903400110

Syal, M. (1997). *Anita and Me*. London, England: Flamingo.

An Interview with Ben Burdett

Hometown: *Pittsford, NY*

Major: *History major, Music minor*

Hobbies: *Playing music, reading, having crazy adventures.*

Do/did you like Geneseo? Why did you choose to come to Geneseo?

Ben: Geneseo's reputation as a high quality liberal arts college is what initially attracted me. I was not sure about exactly what I wanted to do when I came to college, and Geneseo seemed like a place where I could explore some of my various interests while receiving an excellent education. My hometown is only about thirty minutes from Geneseo, which is convenient. I am involved with a lot of different things in Rochester, so being able to go to school close by is helpful. I like that I am a part of two very different yet connected communities. The cost of tuition at Geneseo was also a major selling point.

I like Geneseo very much. I feel that I have developed a lot of great relationships with people that will last for a long time. I have learned so much—inside of the classroom for sure, but also about other things, like how to live and interact with other people. I especially value the creativity of people here. There is a really wonderful music/art/academic community, and people are doing all sorts of creative things that inspire me quite a bit. I feel very fortunate to be around so many intelligent and talented people who care about each other and about fostering an open-minded, creative environment.

Why do you feel that GREAT Day is important?

Many of Geneseo's students are incredibly talented and innovative thinkers, but they do not always receive appropriate acknowledgement. For me, GREAT Day is about recognizing the outstanding work of our peers and commending them on their achievements. Most of us know that we are surrounded by many independent and intelligent people here on campus, and celebrating that is a really special thing that we should be doing on a daily basis. GREAT Day is a nice reminder.

How did it feel to present your work at GREAT Day?

It's a big honor to be able to present at GREAT Day. The amount of effort students put into GREAT Day projects, presentations, and performances is truly remarkable. I am completely amazed by some of the things people are doing here. It honestly sometimes feels like I should not even be in the same company as some of Geneseo's other students, because their work totally eclipses mine on so many levels. We have people doing very inspiring things here, and it is awesome to be a part of a community of people who support each other. It is a great privilege to be a part of GREAT Day.

"Urban Harlequins with Outmoded Fashions": The Use of Record Players by Modern Hipsters

Ben Burdett

For an object, the record player occupies a highly unique place in modern culture. It is a reminder of where music used to be: how it was consumed, how it was manufactured/marketed, and how it was experienced by listeners of the past. Vinyl records and the record player function as a form of nostalgia for the 1950s and 1960s, when vinyl was the dominant medium for music. Recent statistics indicate that vinyl records have been gaining resurgence in popularity; in 2013, vinyl sales increased by 32% in the United States (International Federation of the Phonography Industry, 2014). Scholar Bernardo Alexander Attias (2011) noted that DJs or audiophiles did not drive the resurgence of vinyl records. Attias (2011) attributes the boost in vinyl sales to a unique American subculture: college-educated, middle- and upper-class urban youth, commonly referred to as "hipsters." Today, record players and vinyl have become synonymous with hipsters in popular culture. "Hipsters," as described by one NPR writer, are people who "drink cheap beer, listen to music on vinyl records, and decorate their lairs with up cycled furniture" (Weeks, 2011). The connection between record players and hipsters goes beyond simple association. The record player as an object and image has come to be symbolic of the stereotypical hipster; representative of identity, education, socioeconomic status, and the search for authenticity through nostalgia and irony. The fact that the record player holds such significance for a small percentage of young people may not be important in itself, but understanding how and why the record player holds this significance will shed important light on certain, less obvious aspects of society as a whole—mainly, why objects influence and define certain individuals.

In *Eyewitnessing,* a monograph of European Art, historian Peter Burke (2001) notes that images can help

Figure 1. A record player. via flic.kr/p/fL4jtH by Bill Benzon (CC BY-SA 2.0)

historians gain access to a "history of mentalities" (p. 9), or a sense of how and why people thought differently in the past. Although images are by nature distorted and subjective representations of reality, Burke (2001) states that,

> The process of distortion is itself evidence of phenomena that many historians want to study: mentalities, ideologies, and identities. The material or literal image is good evidence of the mental or metaphorical "image" of the self or of others. (p. 30)

The image of the record player indicates that hipsters (a) have a desire for high-quality music, (b) can afford to purchase a record player and records for it, and (c) find listening to music and acquiring physical musical devices personally significant—as indicated by the private space which the record player/records occupy (the home). Indeed, these assertions are closely related to how hipsters are perceived in 2015; snobbish about music, educated, wealthy, and self-defining through (usually ironic) visual cues. One New York Times journalist described rather bluntly: "The hipster haunts every city street and university town…He tries to negotiate the age-old problem of individuality, not with concepts, but with material things" (Wampole, 2012). The description this journalist provides assumes that hipsters define themselves through material and visual objects. The record player becomes an object through which a person defines their identity. The object, to the hipster, is symbolic of many aspects of his or her life: education, wealth, and desire for authentic music (and authenticity in general). The image of a record player can characterize the hipsters' personalities, both in the eyes of others and also themselves.

If the hipster views the records and the record players as representative of who they are, then the image of the record player can be interpreted as an advertisement for hipsters, selling hipsters an image of themselves. The record player has become a visual representation of the hipster identity and advertisers may use that image/identity to sell a product that the hipster can use to define and to display themselves as individuals. Researcher John Berger (1972) states,

> All publicity works upon anxiety. The sum of everything is money; to get money is to overcome anxiety. Alternatively the anxiety on which publicity plays is the fear that having nothing you will be nothing…The power to spend money is the power to live. According to the legends of publicity, those who lack the power to spend money become literally faceless. Those who have the power become lovable. (p. 143)

The aura created by the record player's image is selling the product; not just the object, but a lifestyle and an identity associated with the object. The image essentially tells the viewer: 'buying this record player will allow you to assert your individuality. It will give you a physical representation of who you are at home, in private (i.e., who you *really* are). Having the ability to purchase records means exercising "freedom of choice" as an individual, and therefore the ability to have an identity. Identity construction is reinforced by the ability to purchase records publicly; one's identity becomes attached to the purchase made in a store. In short, the image of the record player sells hipsters their own image.

An important part of the hipster image that is being marketed to individuals is nostalgia. According to the New York Times journalist Christy Wampole (2012), the hipster is characterized as "manifesting a nostalgia for times he never lived himself…this contemporary urban harlequin appropriates outmoded fashions (the mustache, the tiny shorts), mechanisms (fixed-gear bicycles, portable record players) and hobbies (home brewing, playing trombone)." The record player represents "outmoded fashions," and grants hipsters an identity that can be marketed to others as a part of their "cool" and "unique" personalities, which stand in contrast to the status quo. Therefore, the record player, and specifically the image/aura of it, serves as publicity of one's identity. Furthermore, the fact that the image alludes to the record player as an object of nostalgia is significant, for as John Berger (1972) states,

> Publicity is, in essence, nostalgic. It has to sell the past to the future. It cannot itself supply the standards of its own claims. And so all its references to quality

are bound to be retrospective and traditional. It would lack both confidence and credibility if it used a strictly contemporary language. Publicity needs to turn to its own advantage the traditional education of the average spectator-buyer. What he has learnt at school of history, mythology, poetry can be used in the manufacturing of glamour. (p. 140)

As people are aware of the high quality and price of vinyl music, as well as its role in the history of music, the record player becomes symbolic of "authenticity" and nostalgia. Putting the record player on display as an object that defines one's identity allows the individual to present oneself as "authentic," and nostalgic for a better time period.

One last thing must be noted regarding the central issue surrounding the analysis presented in this paper, and the use of images as historical evidence. Historian Peter Burke (2001) explains that,

It can be extremely misleading to view art as a simple expression of a 'spirit of the age' or *Zeitgeist*. Cultural historians have often been tempted to treat certain images, famous works of art in particular, as representative of the period in which they were produced. Temptations should not always be resisted, but this one has the disadvantage of assuming that historical periods are homogenous enough to be represented by a single picture in this way. (p. 31)

Representing a historical time period with a single image is misleading because the image can never fully capture every dimension of the time period it relates to. The same principle can be applied to the record player (both the image of it and the object itself). Although it has been demonstrated that the record player has become a symbolic object for a certain group of people referred to as hipsters, one must be wary of drawing conclusions from this apparent connection. The branding of people as hipsters is a generalization and stereotype; who exactly qualifies as a hipster is entirely subjective and difficult enough to determine. This is not to say that there is no connection to be made between urban, middle- and upper-class youth and the resurgence of vinyl; as has been shown in this paper, there is in fact a connection to be made. Rather, what is important to remember is that this object/image is not *solely* representative of people classified as hipsters. As an object, the record player functions in a variety of ways for many different people. It can function as nostalgia, a status symbol, or simply a format through which high-quality music can be experienced. Even though owning a record player may be characteristic of hipsters, this is a connection based entirely on stereotype. The identity of an individual cannot be reduced to a single object or image, no matter how tempting or apparently correct it may be.

REFERENCES

Attias, B. A. (2011). Meditations on the death of vinyl. *Dancecult: Journal of Electronic Dance Music Culture, 3*(1). doi:10.12801/1947-5403.2011.03.01.10

Berger, J. (1972). *Ways of seeing.* New York, NY: Penguin Books.

Burke, P. (2001). *Eyewitnessing: The use of images as historical evidence.* Ithaca, NY: Cornell University Press.

International Federation of the Phonography Industry. (2014). *IFPI digital music report 2014.* Retrieved from http://www.ifpi.org/downloads/Digital-Music-Report-2014.pdf

Wampole, C. (2012, November 17). How to live without irony. *New York Times.* Retrieved from http://nyti.ms/U6WVf5

Weeks, L. (2011). The hipsterification of America. *NPR.* Retrieved from http://n.pr/vOwne5

An Interview with Nathalie Grogan

Hometown: *Delmar, NY*

Major: *Double majored in French and History with a minor in International Relations, currently working in ESL education.*

Hobbies: *Dance, hiking, reading.*

Do/did you like Geneseo? Why did you choose to come to Geneseo?

Nathalie: I decided to attend Geneseo after my campus visit in the spring of my senior year of high school. I completely fell in love with the campus, and after talking to many people during my visit, I could envision myself as part of the community. Geneseo`s vast array of study abroad opportunities appealed to me, as well as the core curriculum requirements that had students explore subjects beyond their specialization. I find a broad liberal arts education to be very valuable; I often applied knowledge to other classes and made connections. The strong foreign language department was key in my decision to attend Geneseo, as well as the hundreds of student clubs and organizations that I learned about during my visit.

I cannot say enough good things about my time at Geneseo! I had fabulous professors of History, French, and International Relations who inspired me every day. The organizations that I joined and became a leader of gave me the opportunities to develop myself professionally. Overall, the main component of Geneseo that contributed to my wonderful experience was the student body. I looked up to many of my classmates who did and are doing amazing things—Geneseo is a very special community.

Why do you feel GREAT Day is important?

GREAT Day is important as a showcase of students work—but also of students excellence and independence. GREAT Day projects are voluntary. It is usually a passion project that allows the students' work to shine. Ever since I attended my first GREAT Day as a freshman, I recognized it for how special it was—bringing together students and faculty to pursue academic interests that are purely their own, and not mandated by a class or curriculum.

How did it feel to present your work at GREAT Day?

I felt, above all, grateful for the opportunities I have been able to enjoy at Geneseo. My advisor, Dr. Catherine Adams, was incredibly helpful in my preparation for GREAT Day. I felt proud that I was one of the many talented student presenters that day.

Going Back in Time: The Rolling Back of Women's Rights in New York, 1650–1680

Nathalie Grogan

Before 1664, women in the Dutch colony of New Netherland lived under conditions that contrasted greatly with those of their sisters, who resided in the remainder of the colonial Atlantic coast. The Dutch Colony of New Netherland eventually became New York after the English takeover in 1664. While under Dutch rule, the English law of coverture which declared women "femme covert" upon marriage and resulted in the loss of their legal identities was not practiced (Narrett, 1992, p. 70). Eighteenth-century English judge Sir William Blackstone (1899) laid out the proper role of married women under English law in his *Commentaries on the Laws of England*:

> *by* marriage, the husband and wife are one person in law: that is, the very being or legal existence of the woman is suspended during the marriage, or at least is incorporated and consolidated into that of the husband, under whose wing, protection, and cover, she performs everything; and is therefore, in our law-French a femme-covert…under the protection of her husband, her baron or lord, and her condition during her marriage is called her coverture. (p. 422)

Roman–Dutch law was the standard previously; it had been imported from the northwestern Dutch provinces of Holland and Friesland, along with elements of Dutch culture, such as the education and occupational training of daughters (Catterall & Campbell, 2012, p. 191). The role of women in Dutch society evolved from the European standard of total subordination during the Late Middle Ages; as the economy of the Netherlands took off, women started to be valued as commercial and economic agents (Narrett, 1992, p. 43). Girls were expected to be schooled by the same standards as their brothers. Parental obligations and responsibilities towards their children did not vary with gender. In 1643, New Amsterdam residents Claes Janssen and Catelina Pietersen stated, while declaring their duties to their daughter Aelje Claes, that they were "to clothe her, to send her to school, to let her learn reading and writing and a good trade" (Kilpatrick, 1969, p. 218). Under Roman–Dutch law, unmarried women were granted legal civil rights that were nearly equivalent to those of men. Although women were unable to vote for colonial assemblies and legislatures, this was a far cry from the women's status in New England, the Chesapeake Bay, and the southern colonies (Biemer, 1983, p. 211).

Under the influences of English common law, women living in the English colonies of Connecticut, Rhode Island, Massachusetts, and New Hampshire were entirely subordinate in law, religion, and behavior. While the southern and English middle colonies had legal precedent for a married woman's right to her own estate (Narrett, 1992, p. 71), women in New Netherland enjoyed the right to administer their own property, handle legal transactions, represent themselves in court and sign contracts in their own name and that of their husbands (Catterall & Campbell, 2012, p.195). Women took full advantage of their legal rights in New Netherland; on the eve of the English conquest, 195 debt cases were brought before the Dutch colonial court of New Amsterdam in 1663, and 51% of the cases were made by female plaintiffs (Fernow, 1976, p. 21).

Two of the most significant, impactful differences in the treatment of women under Roman-Dutch law as opposed to English law were property and inheritance rights. Under English law, daughters were routinely eliminated from last wills and testaments, and widows were often evicted from their marriage lands to accommodate stepchildren. In New Netherland, women could own property in their own name, and sign joint contracts with their husbands (Goodfriend,

2005, p. 266). Women generally retained their maiden names upon marriage, in contrast to the English custom (Biemer, 1983, p. 2). In addition, marriage contracts in New Netherland were equal contracts between husband and wife, within which both parties brought assets that remained theirs for the duration of the marriage. Under English rule, the personal affairs of wives were automatically part of the husband's estate (the only estate recognized by the law and authorities). Restrictions surrounding women's activity and legal status tightened in the English charter of 1691 through 1828, when the English concept of coverture was ultimately implemented at its peak (Narrett, 1992, p. 6).

Before the English takeover in 1664, it was common for women to appear in courts of their own accord. Prior to the institution of English common law, the Dutch records of Kingston, Ulster County from 1658-1664 demonstrate female participation in the judicial system was rather mundane and expected. In 1663, Kingston resident Geertruyd Andriesen was sued by her neighbor, Roelof Swartwont Schout, for violating the terms of a local ordinance restricting the manner with which one could harvest fields (Oppenheim, 1912, p. 93). Geertruyd's four violations included using additional unauthorized wagons without a guard and the possession of a gun for self-defense while harvesting alone. The Court of Ulster County required Geertruyd to pay a fine to the county, and to pay Schout in wheat and brandy (Oppenheim, 1912, p. 93). This exchange was indistinguishable from any similar violations in which both plaintiff and defendant were men. Geertruyd Andriesen's husband, Jan Andriesen, was not mentioned—a note that likely would have been made after English common law was introduced. Court records after 1674 typically identified women merely as "wife of—"(P. Christoph & F. Christoph, 1983, p. 2).

After 1674, official records that mentioned women by name were nearly always marriage records. Between 1674 and 1688, papers and documents were issued by English governors of New York Edmund Andros (1674-1683) and Thomas Dongan (1683-1688), and on the occasion of their absence, deputy governor, Anthony Brockholls (1681-1683) dealt with a variety of charges, offenses and processes. These documents ranged from trading licenses, deeds of land ownership, theft, arrest warrants, applications for passports,

witness testimony, and civil lawsuits. Ninety percent of the women mentioned in the documents were brides (P. Christoph & F. Christoph, 1983, p. 100-106). In the rare instances that women were mentioned for alternate reasons, such as the accusation of theft for Rebecca Alberts in 1675 (P. Christoph & F. Christoph, 1983, p. 118) and the issue of travel documentation to Elizabeth Arents and Hannah Boons in 1676 (P. Christoph & F. Christoph, 1983, p. 122), women were referred to as "wife of—" (P. Christoph & F. Christoph, 1983, p. 153).

When Richard Nicolls, the first English colonial governor of New York, guaranteed the surrender of New Amsterdam on August 27, 1664, Governor Pieter Stuyvesant negotiated terms favorable to the Dutch citizens, now under English rule (Welling, 1999, p. 17). The peace settlement established the continuation of religious freedom in New Netherland, along with the preservation of Dutch inheritance law in order to avoid confusion (Narrett, 1992, p. 7), but it did not guarantee that women would maintain their legal rights. Once the English solidified their control over the colony, women gradually receded into the private sphere. Through the imposition of English common law, the mobility available to women in society faded away. The 10 year long conquest and final solidification of English rule in 1674 was characterized by piecemeal changes in the status of women (Narrett, 1992, p. 12). During 1665 in the Court of Assize (English-style temporary civil and criminal courts instituted control over the judiciary of New York), a gender-specific pattern developed. From 1665 to 1674, appearances by women in court records under their own names were marginally less than the appearances under Dutch rule. Court records show that incidents of women appearing in court as witnesses, defendants, plaintiffs or through lawsuits dropped only 15% after the initial takeover in 1664 (P. Christoph & F. Christoph, 1983, p. 130). Women still maintained a strong presence in the colonial court at this time (P. Christoph & F. Christoph, 1983, p. 112). However, by 1674 when English rule was solidified women's appearances in court as individuals were cut by 90% (P. Christoph & F. Christoph, 1983, p. 91-102). When women appeared in court after 1674, they were often represented legally by their husbands, such as the case of Elizabeth Appleby's husband, William Appleby, who represented her as defendant against the lawsuit of Thomas Hunt Jr. in 1675 (P. Christoph & F. Christoph, 1983, p. 185).

In the 17th century, marriages in New Netherland were egalitarian. Marriage customs in New Netherland were brought over from the provinces of Holland and Friesland (Biemer, 1983, p. 1). Dutch women had long had the option of choosing between two different concepts of marriage. The *manus* form of marriage necessitated a subordinate wife who would stay under the guardianship of her husband and lose her legal identity; *Usus* marriages, on the other hand, guaranteed married women the same rights as unmarried women (Biemer, 1983, p. 5). In usus marriages, joint wills were the norm. Since unmarried men and women in the Netherlands enjoyed the same civil and legal rights, usus marriages guaranteed no change in status after marriage. The contract between Brant Peelen and Marritje Pieters in 1643 is a prime example. Both spouses, in this case, had been previously married and widowed. The bride retained her maiden name of Pieters through her first marriage, widowhood, and her second marriage to Brand Peelen. The family name, Pieters, was based off of the father's first name, as was traditional in Dutch law and culture (Narrett, 1992, p. 46). The contract specifies that in case of the death, the surviving spouse is to be granted full use of the marital assets, and upon the death of the surviving spouse, the marital assets are to be distributed equally to sons and daughters resulting from their marriage (*Translation of the Marriage Contract*, n.d). Marritje Pieters made sure to safeguard the inheritance received by her children from their deceased father. She required that her current husband pay his stepchildren interest on any property that he borrowed for longer than four years (*Translation of the Marriage Contract*, n.d). The property brought into the marriage by each spouse became marital property during the lifetime of each spouse. After the death of both husband and wife, the heirs of each individual inherit from their birth parent (*Translation of the Marriage Contract*, n.d).

While it was not widespread for women to own land in their own right prior to the English takeover, it was not rare either. New Amsterdam resident Jane Forbus, was granted a land patent and property ownership by the Dutch colonial director of New Netherland, Willem Kieft, in 1647 (Gehring, 1980, p. 61). This ac-

tion was at odds with the change in inheritance and family law that followed after the implementation of English common law. Under English rule, upon marriage, the property of wives became the property of husbands and was liable to be inherited by the husband's heirs when he died. This situation could cause a widow to be bankrupted by her stepchildren, an incident which was avoided by the careful contract brought up and signed by Brant Peelen and Marritje Pieters in 1643. Wives also maintained the right to distance themselves from their husbands' debts, both during their marriage and after a divorce or death.

Under Roman-Dutch law, wives were never held responsible for repaying their husband's debts regardless of the personal financial relations between husband and wife within marriage; Gravesend resident Sarah Davis was granted "a warrant to protect and keep her harmless from any arrest or trouble upon her husband's account" (P. Christoph & F. Christoph, 1982, p. 526).

By the turn of the century, the rights of married women in New York had been stripped away. Under the English common law precept of coverture, women's identities became one with their husbands, and the husband became the legal representative for their union. The colonial laws of 1710 solidified women's status as on par with that of minors and insane individuals (*Chapter 216*, n.d.). Married women were categorized with "persons under the age of one and twenty years, persons not of sound mind, persons imprisoned or those beyond the seas" (*Chapter 216*, n.d.). All of these classes of people were barred from owning property in their own name, with their assets and property requiring a guardian to make legal decisions. In addition, women, the insane, and prisoners were not permitted to make legal documents or contracts under their own name, thus relegating them all as perpetual children (*Chapter 216*, n.d.). In the case that women maintained their own personal property through antenuptial agreements, English law forbade wives from passing on real estate through a last will and testament; husbands held final consent over the inheritance of his wife's personal belongings (Narrett, 1992, p. 17). As a result of English common law, women lost their adulthood and autonomy upon marriage.

During Dutch rule, women were granted the ability to rise to prominent places in the New Netherland society. For women residing in any of the other Atlantic colonies, the ability to rise was nearly impossible. Businesswomen in New Netherland thrived by expanding commercial empires, facilitating enterprise across the Atlantic, and acting as partners to their husbands. The lives of wealthy white women such as Deborah Moody (1586-1659), Margaret Hardenbroeck (1631-1691), Maria van Renssalaer (1645-1689), and Alida Schuyler Livingston (1656-1727) were atypical of average women in the colony by dint of their opportunities and resources. However, women's positions at the helm of key industries and political dynasties served as a message about the value of women in New Netherland. The presence of women such as Margaret Hardenbroeck was indicative of a society in which women were expected and welcomed in the business world. Lady Hardenbroeck was able to rise in the communities of New Netherland and New York because of her wealth, but the society that allows women to be business tycoons is built on small businesses of middle-class women. Political dynasties and leaders such as Maria van Renssalaer, Alida Schuyler Livingston, and Deborah Moody were out of the reach of average women and men in the colony but were envisioned by a society in which women and men were permitted to exercise their talents to improve their lives and standing (Biemer, 1983, p. 85-90).

An exceptional woman from New Netherland of English nobility was Deborah Moody, née Dunch. Born in 1585 to wealthy parents in Wiltshire, England, Deborah Dunch married Henry Moody in 1606. As the wife of a Member of Parliament, she became an influential and well-respected woman, in spite of her devout Anabaptist faith (Biemer, 1983, p. 11). Moody was widowed in 1629, and emigrated to and settled in Massachusetts Bay Colony in 1639 after being driven out of London and her native England by religious persecution from the government. Due to her social status and her friendship with Governor John Winthrop, she was awarded 400 acres of land. However, once again, she found herself in the religious minority in the pious puritan community of Lynn, Massachusetts. In 1643 Moody settled in New Netherland because of the colony's tolerant nature (Biemer, 1983, p. 13). She became the only 17th cen-

tury European woman to found a town as the leader of Gravesend, on present-day Long Island. A lifetime of religious persecution prompted Moody to insert as much religious freedom and liberty of conscience as possible into the charter of Gravesend, which persisted until her death in 1659 (Biemer, 1983, p. 31). Even in the relatively liberal New Netherland, Moody's leadership in her community, regardless of her inability to vote for the councilors she presided over, was unique. Moody's opportunity to live independently and manage the affairs of a town was only made possible because she resided in New Netherland and under Roman-Dutch Law.

Margaret Hardenbroeck, a remarkable woman of New Netherland, established herself as a trader and businesswoman in her own right under Roman-Dutch law. After the death of her first husband Pieter deVries in 1661, Margaret inherited his business. She made many transatlantic voyages, dealing primarily with furs and finished products, as part of her work in trading and business (Catterall & Campbell, 2012, p. 183). After her remarriage to Frederick Philipse in 1663, Margaret continued her business until she was phased out of control by the implementation of English common law in 1674. Within five years of the English takeover, the ability of wives to grant power of attorney to their husbands was abolished, eliminating the business partnership Margaret and her husband had built throughout their marriage (Biemer, 1983, p. 37). Margaret remained a key figure in trading until her death in 1691, but her later years (1674-1691) were ones during which her husband was able to assert control over her affairs (Biemer, 1983, p. 6). Margaret's career is a prime example of the consequences of English law; it showed the rise and fall of women's rights in New Netherland and New York.

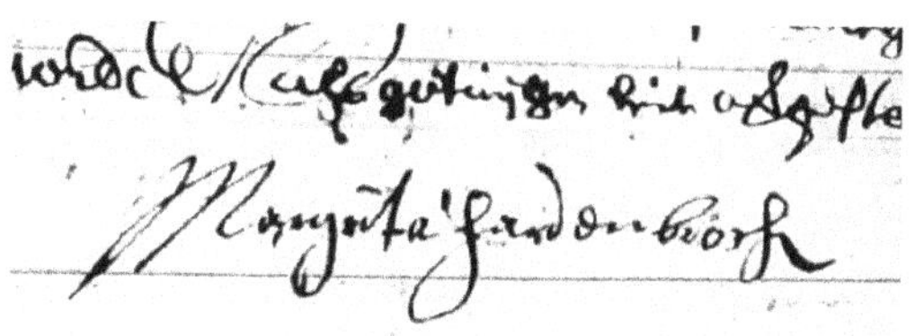

Figure 1: Official signature of Margaret Hardenbroeck to acknowledge personal debt in 1664. (Zimmerman, 2006)

Maria van Renssalaer, née van Cortlandt, was notable as a distinguished administrator of the patroonship (manorial landholding) of Renssalaerswyck, New Netherland, after the English takeover. Born to a prominent and wealthy family of colonial traders and politicians, young Maria learned to manage her father's brewery at an early age. Her marriage in 1662 to Jeremias van Renssalaer—the director of Renssalaerswyck and a member of the high profile Renssalaer dynasty— was a partnership within which she was an active player (Biemer, 1983, p. 46). Maria's business experience managed to save the familial and neglected Renssalaerswyck Manor from bankruptcy (Biemer, 1983, p. 47). However, the gradual introduction of English law meant that as a married woman—and eventually a widow—Maria was barred from assuming traditional directing roles for the patroonship. Her brother, Stephanus van Cortlandt, ran the manor in name following the death of his brother-in-law, Jeremias, in 1674. The 10 years between the initial English takeover and the solidification of their rule in 1674 emphasized a clear loss of Maria's powers over the estate (Biemer, 1983, p. 50). Nevertheless, while Maria was not director of the manor in name, she was courted by New York political leaders for patronage and favors, and was widely recognized as the force behind the manor (Biemer, 1983, p. 52). Visitors to the manor referred to Maria as "Madam Renssalaer" (Renssalaer, 1935). She presided over the most prosperous years of the Renssalaerswyck manor and defied the expected role of women under the restrictive English laws (Biemer, 1983, p. 53).

Alida Schuyler Livingston was born in 1656 at Fort Orange. She was a uniquely influential woman in New Netherland. As daughter of recent Dutch immigrants and prominent fur traders Philip Peterse Schuyler and Margaretta Van Schlechtenhorst, Alida Schuyler knew of the power women held in New Netherland firsthand; her mother Margaretta managed the family estate from her widowhood in 1683 until her death in 1701 (Biemer, 1982, p. 184). Alida Schuyler married Robert Livingston in 1679 and entered, as was close as possible in 17th century New Netherland, into an equal marriage (Biemer, 1982, p. 185). The Livingston business of land, public office, and textile trade propelled the couple to be considered the elite of New York by the 1720s (Biemer, 1982, p. 187). Correspondence between Alida and Robert Livingston over the course of the 48 year-long marriage indicates that theirs was a partnership. Letters from Alida to Robert indicate affection as well as business inquiries and transactional details from merchants and clients, including exact figures, quantities, and prices (Biemer, 1982, p.189). In a letter dated August 25, 1698, well after the English takeover of New Netherland, Alida instructed her husband to check the list of available goods from Holland and warned him about a poor crop of wheat due to heavy rains. In addition, the letter informed her husband that she had taken it upon herself to negotiate business for him with the current recorder of Albany (Biemer, 1982, p. 194).

Deborah Moody, Margaret Hardenbroeck, Maria van Renssalaer, and Alida Schuyler Livingston enjoyed recognition far beyond what was extended to women across the Atlantic coast. However, middle-class and working-class women in New Netherland also benefited from Roman–Dutch law. Teuntje Straatmans was born in the Netherlands in 1616. She briefly ruled the colony of New Holland in present-day Brazil before settling in New Amsterdam during the year of 1655 (Cramer van der Bogaart, 2003, p. 40). Upon her wedding to Belgian merchant Gabriel Corbesij in 1657, Teuntje agreed to the usus form of marriage, retained her maiden name, and signed an antenuptial agreement detailing her legal and civil rights (Cramer van der Bogaart, 2003, p. 42). Following her marriage, Teuntje Straatmans appears in the records of New Amsterdam several times, in civil lawsuits and property disputes among neighbors. In 1658 she was obliged to defend herself in court against accusations of belligerence from her neighbor Pieter Jansen, and she was subsequently fined by the local court (Cramer van der Bogaart, 2003, p. 43). Their family home on the island of present-day Manhattan was recorded as "owned by Teuntje Straatmans and her husband" (Cramer van der Bogaart, 2003), a note which revealed that the property was under her name. Her ability to move through society and her lifetime independently, regardless of her marital status, was not due to her socioeconomic status but the legal code of her community.

The shift in women's status and rights in colonial New Netherland and New York challenges the historical narrative of civil rights as a progressive force. Throughout history, the franchise and civil rights have been expanded slowly but clearly. Very rarely have rights been rolled back. The change in power and authority in New York brought in a new monarch, new representatives of the royal authority, new councils and judicial systems, and a new legal basis for legislation. Additionally, it becomes clear that cultural views regarding individuals roles in society vary in accordance with which nation is the colonizer. The standards of gender equality present in New Netherland had a source: the cultural norms of their country of origin, the Netherlands. In 17th century Amsterdam, girls were educated to the same degree as their brothers, with the expectation of learning a trade, completing an apprenticeship and contributing to the family income through outside work and businesses. In contrast, prior to the Industrial Revolution in England, women were primarily charged with domestic work. Lower-income women in England certainly worked for wages in order to keep their families afloat, but it was middle-class women in the Netherlands who drove for the education of daughters.

The basis for the unique situation of women in New Netherland evolved from the cultural understanding that women and girls were equally capable of business work and of understanding laws. This cultural attitude towards women extended towards property ownership and marriage rights. New Netherland, as a society which valued the contribution of women to the local economy, had laid the foundations for the legal and civil rights enjoyed by female residents. Based off of the cultural narrative of the Netherlands, women participated as full economic actors. It was beneficial for the colony to allow women social and civil opportunities which worked to enrich the community.

Influential women such as Alida Schuyler Livingston, Maria van Rensselaer, Margaret Hardenbroeck, and Deborah Moody are representative of the freedoms women enjoyed in New Netherland and New York. The English takeover in 1664 and the final implementation of English common law in 1674 worked towards rolling back women's participation in the community as individuals, and while women such as the aforementioned leaders managed to hold on to their current businesses, younger women were denied the opportunity to polish their business acu-

men and engage themselves. This fact created disastrous results for themselves and the community.

The change of rule from Dutch to English caused women to be shut out of the legal economy, pushing many to illegal means as a way of supporting themselves and their families. In New Amsterdam Dutch women committed 0.664% of crimes from the years 1640-1670, but in the years of solid English rule from 1691-1776, women accounted for 16.3% of all crimes committed (Biemer, 1983, p. 3). The rise of women involved in the black market of prostitution or smuggling in New York was not unexpected after it was established that women were unable to secure business or trading licenses from the English governor. As the population of New Netherland and New York had been mostly made up of working-class immigrants, the cultural tradition of women owning businesses did not contribute to a uniquely wealthy colony. Tellingly, once women were barred under English common law from obtaining many of the trading licenses available to them under the Dutch, average family incomes plummeted (Biemer, 1983, p. 52).

However, not every aspect of radical Dutch thought and behavior was eradicated upon the English conquest. Girls were still routinely educated alongside boys after 1674; the education of daughters was often included in family directives and wills. Albany resident Cornelius von Bursam wrote to his wife on his deathbed in 1680 about his daughter (her stepdaughter): "She is to maintain my daughter Anna decently, and cause her, being taught reading and writing and a trade by which she may live" (Kilpatrick, 1969, p. 219). Although the colonial government of New York was opposed to reinstating the rights of women to represent themselves in court, participate in the local economy, and own property, the cultural landscape of New York remained built on legal and civil rights.

The narrative of women's rights in New York does not follow the standard map towards social change. The advancement of Dutch culture contributed to the progression of civil rights for women, and was exported through colonialism into New Netherland. During Dutch rule, New Netherland displayed countless examples of women participating in the local economy and judicial system, with cases ranging from self-defense, civil lawsuits, widowhood, and land ownership. The rejection of standard Western European systems of coverture left Dutch women free to assume and develop legal identities independent of their husbands, families or marital status. The accomplishments and power of influential leaders such as Deborah Moody, Alida Schuyler Livingston, Margaret Hardenbroeck, and Maria van Renssalaer demonstrated the capabilities of women to use their legal freedoms to build careers and rise to prominence. Restrictions placed upon Maria Van Renssalaer's ability to manage her familial estate once English common law was established exposed the consequences of the regime change on prominent women. The life of Teuntje Straatsmans highlights the significance of a judicial and legal system that aims to empower citizens rather than restrict their lives. The regime change in 1664 brought a new monarch in King Charles II, and relatively few internal political changes due to the negotiations of Pieter Stuyvesant. However, the lives of the women in the colony, and the make-up of New Netherland and New York, were altered by the English takeover. Married women, subsumed into the identity of their husbands, gradually lost their cherished rights. Their opportunities to manage their own affairs, properties, and businesses were taken away and they themselves shut out of the developing economy that was run under the control of the English.

REFERENCES

Blackstone, W. (1899). *Commentaries on the laws of England.* J.D. Andrews (Ed.). Chicago, IL: Callaghan and Co.

Biemer, L.B. (Trans.). (1982). Business letters of Alida Schuyler Livingston, 1680-1726. *New York History, 63*(2), 182-207.

Biemer, L. B. (1983). *Women and property in colonial New York: The transition from Dutch to English law, 1643-1727.* Ann Arbor, MI: UMI Research Press.

Catterall, D., & Campbell, J. (Eds.). (2012). *Women in port: Gendering communities, economies, and social networks in Atlantic port cities, 1500-1800.* Boston, MA: Brill.

Chapter 216 of colonial laws [Transcript] (n.d.). Retrieved from http://nysa32.nysed.gov/education/showcase/201001women/activities_dbq3.shtml#translation

Christoph, P. R., & Christoph F. A. (Eds.). (1982). *New York historical manuscripts, English: Books of general entries of the colony of New York, 1664-1673.* Baltimore, MD: Genealogical Publishing Co., Inc.

Christoph, P. R., & Christoph F. A. (Eds.). (1983). *New York historical manuscripts, English: Records of the Court of Assizes for the colony of New York, 1665-1682.* Baltimore, MD: Genealogical Publishing Co., Inc.

Cramer van den Bogaart, A. (2003). The life of Teuntje Straatmans: A Dutch woman's travels in the seventeenth century Atlantic world. *Long Island Historical Journal, 15*(2), 35-53.

Fernow, B. (Ed.). (1976). *The records of New Amsterdam from 1653 to 1674.* Baltimore, MD: Genealogical Publishing Co., Inc.

Furer, H.B. (Ed.). (1974). *New York: A chronological and documentary history, 1524-1970.* Dobbs Ferry, NY: Oceana Publications, Inc.

Gehring, C. T. (Ed.). (1980). *New York historical manuscripts, Dutch: Land papers.* Baltimore, MD: Genealogical Publishing Co., Inc.

Goodfriend, J. D. (Ed.). (2005). *Revisiting New Netherland: Perspectives on early Dutch America.* Boston, MA: Brill.

Kilpatrick, W. H. (1969). *The Dutch schools of New Netherland and colonial New York.* New York, NY: Arno Press & The New York Times.

Narrett, D. E. (1992). *Inheritance and family life in colonial New York City.* Ithaca, NY: Cornell University Press.

Oppenheim, S. (Ed. & Trans.). (1912). *The Dutch records of Kingston, Ulster county 1658-1664.* Cooperstown, NY: New York State Historical Association Publishers.

Renssalaer, M. V. (1935). *Correspondence of Maria Van Renssalaer, 1669-1689*. A. F. J Van Laer (Ed. & Trans.). Albany, NY: SUNY Albany Press.

Translation of the marriage contract between Brant Peelen and Marritje Pieters, widow of Claes PIetersen [Translation]. (n.d.). Retrieved from http://nysa32.nysed.gov/education/showcase/201001women/trans_peelen.shtml

Welling, G. R. (1999). *The United States of America and the Netherlands*. Boston, MA: Brill Academic Publishers.

Zimmerman, J. (2006). *The women of the house: How a colonial she-merchant built a mansion, a fortune, and a dynasty*. Orlando, FL: Harcourt Books, Inc.

Further Reading

Christoph, P. R., & Christoph F. A. (Eds.). (1982). *New York historical manuscripts, English: Books of general entries of the colony of New York, 1674-1688*. Baltimore, MD: Genealogical Publishing Co., Inc.

Christoph, P. R., Scott, K., & Stryker-Rodda, K., (Eds.). (1976). *New York historical manuscripts, Dutch: Kingston Papers* (Vols. 1-2). Baltimore, MD: Genealogical Publishing Co., Inc.

Gehring, C. T. (Ed.). (2000). *Correspondence, 1647-1653*. Syracuse, NY: Syracuse University Press.

Gehring, C. T. (Ed.). (2003). *Correspondence, 1654-1658*. Syracuse, NY: Syracuse University Press.

Gehring, C. T. (Ed.). (1995). *Council minutes, 1655-1656*. Syracuse, NY: Syracuse University Press.

Gehring, C. T. (Ed.). (2000). *Fort Orange records, 1656-1678*. Syracuse, NY: Syracuse University Press.

Gehring, C. T. (Ed.). (1991). *Laws and writs of appeals, 1647-1663*. Syracuse, NY: Syracuse University Press.

Gehring, C. T. (Ed.). (1983). *New York historical manuscripts, Dutch: Council minutes, 1652-1654*. Baltimore, MD: Genealogical Publishing Co., Inc.

Gehring, C. T., & Zeller-McClure, N.A. (Eds.). (1985). *Education in New Netherland and the middle colonies: Papers of the 7th Renssalaerswyck seminar of the New Netherland project*. Interlaken, NY: Heart of the Lakes Publishing.

O'Callaghan, E.B. (Ed.). (1850). *Papers relating to the first settlement of New York by the Dutch*. Albany, NY: Weed, Parsons and Co., Public Printers.

An Interview with Kate Hesler

Hometown: *Mahopac, NY*

Major: *Psychology and English Literature*

Hobbies: *Piano, tennis, reading, Netflixing!*

Do/did you like Geneseo? Why did you choose to come to Geneseo?

Kate: Geneseo drew me in for its academic rigor, liberal arts focus, and warm atmosphere. Of course, I also fell in love with Geneseo's beautiful scenery! It was always high on my list of prospective colleges, but my decision to attend Geneseo was confirmed for me when I went to an accepted students overnight visit. I was surprised to see strangers smiling at me and greeting hello wherever I went. I decided to pursue my undergraduate degree at Geneseo because the college made me feel welcome, and I could envision myself there are a student.

Attending Geneseo is the best decision that I have made in my life. It is a place where I discovered alot about myself and that absolutely changed how I see the world. I also formed the most amazing friendships at Geneseo. Since graduating, I miss Geneseo every single day. It truly became my home away from home.

Why do you feel that GREAT Day is important?

The students at Geneseo are amazingly talented and have definitely made some fantastic achievements. GREAT Day is a phenomenal opportunity for Geneseo students to showcase their academic accomplishments and creative work. I loved attending GREAT Day as a Geneseo student because it was always really astounding for me to see all the work that students and departments accomplish each year.

How did it feel to present your work at GREAT day?

Presenting at GREAT Day last year left me with some mixed feelings. I was excited to talk to the Geneseo students and faculty about my research on perfectionism and social anxiety in college students, but I was also nervous about public speaking in front of a large group of people. However, I am really grateful to my wonderful friends who allowed me to practice in front of them multiple times. After my presentation, I felt proud that I was able to share my research with the Geneseo community.

Perfectionism, Social Support, and Social Anxiety in College Students

Kate Hesler

ABSTRACT

The study examined the role of socially prescribed perfectionism on social anxiety and perfectionistic self-presentation behaviors in college students. One hundred twenty-nine students at a public liberal arts college completed questionnaires assessing their trait perfectionism, perfectionistic self-presentation, social anxiety, and perceived social support. The results found direct relationships between socially prescribed perfectionism and social anxiety, and between socially prescribed perfectionism and perfectionistic self-presentation. The results indicate conceptual, although not statistically significant, evidence for social support moderating the relationship between socially prescribed perfectionism and social anxiety. There was neither conceptual nor statistical support for a social support interaction on the association between socially prescribed perfectionism and perfectionistic self-presentation. The findings suggest that perfectionistic college students are likely to engage in maladaptive impression management behaviors. College students who strive for perfection to please others and who have low levels of social support may also be at risk of developing social anxiety.

PURPOSE

Social anxiety disorder is one of the most common mental health problems for college students in the United States and affects 15 million American adults (Anxiety and Depression Association of America, 2010). Social anxiety disorder is the fear of social interaction, including the fear of being evaluated or judged. Since the transition from living at home with parents while in high school to living surrounded by peers while at college involves a significant uprooting from an individual's life, students are quite vulnerable to the stresses of college. Social anxiety is a serious problem for undergraduates because it is often associated with other mental disorders, such as depression (Kuzel, 1996) and alcohol dependency (Schry & White, 2013). Social anxiety is also associated with several cognitive behaviors and effects such as stress (Smith, Ingram, & Brehm, 1983), procrastination (Frost, Marten, Lahart, & Rosenblate, 1990), and personality traits like perfectionism (Flett, Endler, Tassone, & Hewitt, 1994; Hewitt & Flett, 1991).

In the present study, the goal is to determine whether perfectionistic students may be at risk of developing social anxiety during college and whether perfectionism is associated with certain maladaptive behaviors. This will involve examining how social support moderates such a relationship between perfectionism and social anxiety, and between perfectionism and perfectionistic behaviors. Perhaps the relationship between perfectionism and social anxiety and the relationship between perfectionism and unhealthy behaviors is most problematic for students lacking significant social support at college. The question at hand, therefore, has to do with the factors affecting the perfectionism, perfectionistic behaviors, and social anxiety in college students.

LITERATURE REVIEW

Perfectionism Defined

Hewitt and Flett (1991) suggest perfectionism is a personality trait that can occasionally be a positive factor in adjustment and achievement but is predominantly viewed as a "pervasive neurotic style" (p. 456). Adjustment difficulties of perfectionism include setting exact and unrealistic standards, striving to attain such standards, overgeneralization of failure, critical self-evaluations, and "a tendency to engage in all-or-none thinking whereby only total success or total failure exists as outcomes" (Hewitt & Flett, 1991, p. 456). Perfectionism has been associated with various negative outcomes like feelings of failure, shame, and low self-esteem. Perfectionism has been linked to several forms of psychopathology like alcoholism (Hewitt, Norton, Flett, Callander, & Cowan, 1999), depression (Flett et al., 1994), narcissistic personality (Watson, Varnell, & Morris, 1999), and suicidal ideation (Hewitt, Flett, & Weber, 1999).

Domains of Perfectionism

Perfectionism is a multidimensional construct and can be either adaptive or maladaptive (Dunkley, Blankstein, Halsall, Williams, & Winkworth, 2000; Terry-Short, Glynn Owen, Slade, & Dewey, 1995; Hewitt & Flett, 1991). Perfectionism can be both positive, in which perfectionism relates to achievement and positive consequences, and negative (or neurotic), in which perfectionism is a function of avoiding negative consequences (Terry-Short et al., 1995). Dunkley et al. (2000) suggest that perfectionism can be broken down into personal standards perfectionism, resembling the adaptive type, and evaluative concerns perfectionism, resembling the maladaptive type. According to a 1990 study by Hewitt and Flett, adaptive perfectionism includes positive perfectionistic behaviors, such as setting high standards that match an individual's limitations and strengths and engaging in balanced thinking (as cited in Hewitt & Flett, 1991). Adaptive perfectionism can be indicated by standards and order, organization, and personal standards (Dunkley et al., 2000). The aforementioned 1990 study by Hewitt and Flett also states that maladaptive perfectionism creates maladjustment in perfectionistic individuals who exercise inflexibly high standards beyond normal expectations, determine their self-worth based on their performance, and engage in total thinking of their performance as either perfection or failure (as cited in Hewitt & Flett, 1991).

Hewitt and Flett (1991) propose three domains, or traits, of perfectionism: self-oriented perfectionism, other-oriented perfectionism, and socially prescribed perfectionism. Self-oriented perfectionism is closely related to personal standards perfectionism and involves several self-directed perfectionistic behaviors like setting exact standards and critical self-evaluation (Hewitt & Flett, 1991; Dunkley et al., 2000). It should be noted that self-oriented perfectionism demonstrates both positive and negative perfectionistic behavior (Dunkley et al., 2000; Hewitt & Flett, 1991). Other-oriented perfectionism involves inter-personal perfectionistic behaviors directed from the individual toward significant others; these perfectionists, therefore, set exact standards for others, place importance on others being perfect, and stringently evaluate others (Hewitt & Flett, 1991). Socially prescribed perfectionism involves the perceived need to attain exact standards and expectations to be perfect prescribed by others. In an article published in 1993, Frost et al. state that socially prescribed perfectionism is the most maladaptive form of perfectionism and is the most related to psychopathology (as cited in Saboonchi & Lundh, 1997); it is associated with evaluative concerns perfectionism when perfectionists engage in concern over making mistakes, doubt about the quality of their actions and performance, and concern about other people's evaluations and criticism of them (Dunkley et al., 2000).

Perfectionistic self-presentation is another maladaptive form of perfectionism since it demonstrates an interpersonal personality style that is pervasive and persistent (Hewitt et al., 2003). Buss and Finn report that perfectionistic self-presentation involves an individual's expression of perfectionistic behavior (as cited in Hewitt et al., 2003). There are individual differences among perfectionists in terms of their levels of trait perfectionism on self-oriented, other-oriented, and socially prescribed dimensions but also in terms of the need to appear perfect and avoid imperfection to other people in public situations. Certain perfectionists engage in impression management involving "self-presentational attempts to create an image of perfection in public situations," or an ideal public self (Hewitt et al., 2003, p. 1303). Hewitt et al. (2003) propose that perfectionistic self-presentation can help distinguish salient differences between individuals who demonstrate similar levels of trait dimensions of perfectionism. Despite scholars such as Schlenker and Weigold who suggest both positive and negative aspects of perfectionistic self-presentation (as cited in Hewitt et al., 2003), Hewitt et al. (2003) maintain that perfectionistic self-presentation is associated with interpersonal and personal distress for the perfectionist.

The three facets of perfectionistic self-presentation are perfectionistic self-promotion, nondisplay of imperfection, and nondisclosure of imperfection (Hewitt et al., 2003). Perfectionistic self-promotion involves the active proclamation and display of one's perfection through one's attempts to look perfect, demonstrate perfection, or behave perfectly to others. Nondisplay of imperfection is the avoidance of and concern about appearing imperfect to others. Similarly, nondisclosure of imperfection involves the avoidance of verbally disclosing perceived personal imperfections and negative attributes. Hewitt et al. (2003) maintain that perfectionistic self-presentation is "pathologically driven and interpersonally aversive" (p. 1305).

Trait Perfectionism and Perfectionistic Self-Presentation

Previous research has found support for the relation between trait perfectionism and perfectionistic self-presentation. Hewitt et al. (2003) found that socially prescribed perfectionism and self-oriented perfectionism are highly associated with perfectionistic self-presentation. The facets of perfectionistic self-promotion and nondisplay of imperfection in perfectionistic self-presentation were found to be related to trait perfectionism; the highest association was found to be between socially prescribed perfectionism and nondisplay of imperfection. The finding may suggest that perfectionists' unwillingness to reveal mistakes could potentially be derived from the perception of others as being critical and demanding perfection. A recent study also demonstrated that high socially prescribed perfectionism predicts facets of perfectionistic self-presentation, particularly perfectionistic self-promotion and nondisclosure of imperfection (Stoeber & Roche, 2014).

Mediators of Perfectionism and Perfectionistic Self-Presentation

Few studies have investigated how certain factors explain the association between socially prescribed perfectionism and perfectionistic self-presentation, but no current studies have investigated how certain factors affect and change the relationship. One study found that negative problem solving ability mediates the relationship between socially prescribed perfectionism and perfectionistic self-presentation in women with depression symptoms (Besser, Flett, & Hewitt, 2010). The findings suggest that socially prescribed perfectionists are unwilling to admit to mistakes after having difficulty solving problems. Interestingly, perfectionistic impression management

behaviors have been found to affect the relationship between perfectionism derived from the need to please others and cognitions about changing one's appearance; perfectionistic self-promotion and nondisplay of imperfection have been found to mediate the relationship between socially prescribed perfectionism and thoughts about having cosmetic surgery performed in undergraduates and individuals who go to the gym (Sherry, Hewitt, Lee-Baggley, Flett, & Besser, 2004). Perfectionists seem to attempt to appease others by boasting perfection and downplaying imperfection but still feel the need to change their appearance despite their impression management behaviors.

Perfectionism and Social Anxiety

Past research has indicated the significant relationship between perfectionism and anxiety/depression (Flett et al., 1994; Hewitt & Flett, 1991). People with adaptive perfectionism demonstrate the lowest levels of anxiety compared to those with maladaptive perfectionism (Gnilka, Ashby, & Noble, 2012).

Other studies have found an association between perfectionism and social anxiety. Historically, social anxiety has been proposed to be related to self-presentation (Schlenker & Leary, 1982). Recent studies have found a link between social anxiety and perfectionistic self-presentation (Jain & Sudhir, 2010; Mackinnon, Battista, Sherry, & Stewart, 2014; Nepon, Flett, Hewitt, & Molnar, 2011). Moreover, social anxiety has also been found to be related to trait perfectionism, specifically socially prescribed perfectionism, in college undergraduates (Laurenti, Bruch, & Haase, 2008; Nepon et al., 2011, Saboonchi & Lundh, 1997). Saboonchi and Lundh (1997) found that perfectionistic dimensions, such as concern over mistakes and doubt about actions, are also related to social anxiety.

Moderators and Mediators of Perfectionism and Social Anxiety

Some research has investigated how various factors affect the relation between perfectionism and psychological distress. Negative and positive coping styles have been found to partially mediate the relationship between maladaptive perfectionism and depression (Zhang & Cai, 2012). The findings suggest that people with high levels of maladaptive perfectionism engage in negative coping styles (such as avoiding problems) more frequently than positive coping styles (such as seeking the help of others). The study's findings support previous research that avoidant coping partially explains the connection between maladaptive perfectionism and distress (Dunn, Whelton, & Sharpe, 2006). One study found evaluative concerns perfectionists with high levels of daily hassles had more feelings of psychological distress symptoms like depression and anxiety than perfectionists with low levels of daily stressors (Dunkley et al., 2000).

One study investigated perfectionism as a moderator of the relationship between self-efficacy in interpersonal situations and social anxiety (Laurenti et al., 2008). The discrepancy between people's perceptions of their social self-efficacy—an estimate of one's own abilities in an interpersonal social situation—and others' perceptions of an individual's social competence relates to socially prescribed perfectionism and social anxiety. People with high levels of socially prescribed perfectionism and social anxiety have high discrepancies that suggest these individuals perceive social situations differently than individuals without high levels of perfectionism and anxiety. Specifically, socially anxious individuals with higher levels of trait perfectionism have greater degrees of maladaptive appraisal of interpersonal situations.

Trait Perfectionism, Perfectionistic Self-Presentation, Social Anxiety, and Social Support

Perceived social support is the perception that an individual has a social network of people from which he or she can receive emotional care and assistance. Social support, particularly low social support, may play a role in the relationship between perfectionism and social anxiety, since other studies have found that positive interpersonal behaviors like social self-efficacy affect the relationship between maladaptive perfectionism and psychological distress (Laurenti et al., 2008). Social support may also play a role in the association between trait perfectionism and perfectionistic impression management behaviors. Perfectionists with high levels of social support may feel less inclined to promote perfection and avoid admitting or revealing imperfection to people who provide them with emotional support even when the perfec-

tionist is not perfect. Perfectionists with low levels of social support may be inclined to engage in impression management if they do not perceive themselves as having a supportive social network.

Perfectionists who try to be perfect for other people and who have low social support may be predisposed to developing social anxiety and may engage in perfectionistic self-presentation behaviors. Social support has been found to be linked to several domains of perfectionism, such as socially prescribed perfectionism (Flett, Druckman, Hewitt, & Wekerle, 2012; Sherry, Law, Hewitt, Flett, & Besser, 2008), evaluative concerns perfectionism (Dunkley et al., 2000), and positive and negative perfectionism (Zhou, Zhu, Zhang, & Cai, 2013). Although perfectionistic self-presentation has not been found to be related to social support, self-presentation has been associated with social support (Li, Kou, & Gao, 2010). Honest self-presentation has a positive effect on social support (Kim & Lee, 2001). Another study found that college students had less social support when they engaged in protective forms of self-presentation (Jackson, Fritch, Nagasaka, & Gunderson, 2002). Several studies have also demonstrated the direct relationship between perceived social support and social anxiety (Calsyn, Winter, & Burger, 2005; Wonderlich-Tierney & Vander Wal, 2010).

Social Support as a Moderator of Perfectionism, Social Anxiety, and Self-Presentation

Although several variables have been demonstrated to affect the relationship between perfectionism and social anxiety, perceived social support has only been investigated in a few studies. Those studies have found perceived social support as a mediator and as a moderator on the association between psychological distress, like depression and anxiety, and perfectionism (Dunkley et al., 2000; Sherry et al., 2008; Zhou et al., 2013).

One study found that low perceived social support explains the association between evaluative concerns perfectionism and high levels of social anxiety (Dunkley et al., 2000). The study suggests that perfectionists who express concern about being evaluated by others are likely to have less social support and more maladjustment than perfectionists with high levels of social support. Individuals with high socially prescribed perfectionism may behave in ways which attract less social support, since such perfectionism is linked to the tendency to conceal perceived imperfections from others (Hewitt et al., 2003; Sherry et al., 2008). Socially prescribed perfectionists may avoid verbal disclosures of personal distress, which might elicit social support from others.

High perceived social support, therefore, may have a protective effect in preventing perfectionists from experiencing anxiety. But few studies have investigated perceived social support as affecting the relationship between perfectionism and social anxiety, although there are obvious benefits of doing so since socially anxious individuals fear social interactions due to the concern over being evaluated or judged. Perfectionists who place great value on appearing perfect for others, or socially prescribed perfectionists, and who have little social support may be at risk to develop social anxiety.

Additionally, social support may also be protective in preventing perfectionists from engaging in maladaptive perfectionistic impression management behaviors. No studies have investigated social support as moderating the relationship between trait perfectionism and perfectionistic self-presentation. Yet, socially prescribed perfectionists with little social support may be more likely to engage in perfectionistic self-presentation than perfectionists with great social support. Perfectionists may be less inclined to manage their behavior if they perceive themselves has having a social network that supports them whether they are perfect or not. The current study will thus assess college students' self-reported trait perfectionism, perfectionistic self-presentation, social support, and social anxiety.

HYPOTHESIS

The present study will investigate the role of the perfectionism's domains on social anxiety. It is hypothesized that socially prescribed perfectionism will be positively related to social anxiety and perfectionistic self-presentation. It is further expected that the effect of socially prescribed perfectionism on social anxiety and on perfectionistic self-presentation will be stronger among college students with low levels of perceived social support. Perfectionists who try

to be perfect to appease others with little social support may be more likely to develop social anxiety and engage in perfectionistic self-presentation behaviors than perfectionists with great social support.

METHOD

Participants

A total of 129 undergraduate students (75.2% female, M = 19.07) from a public liberal arts college in the northeastern United States participated in the study. Participants were primarily Caucasian (70.5%). Participants also identified as African-American (6.2%), Hispanic (7.8%), Asian (10.9%), or other (4.7%). Participants included first-year students (51.2%), sophomores (31.0%), juniors (8.5%), and seniors (9.3%). Students were awarded with extra credit in psychology courses for participating in the study and provided informed consent prior to completing the online survey.

Measures

Socially prescribed perfectionism. The Multidimensional Perfectionism Scale (MPS) was used to assess participants' socially prescribed perfectionism (Hewitt & Flett, 1991). The MPS is a scale used to measure self-oriented perfectionism, other-oriented perfectionism, and socially prescribed perfectionism. The present study used the socially prescribed perfectionism subscale (SPPS) and the self-oriented perfectionism subscale (SOPS) from the MPS. Socially prescribed perfectionism involves "the perceived need to attain standards and expectations prescribed by significant others" (Hewitt & Flett, 1991, p. 457). The SPPS contains fifteen items and includes samples items, such as, "I find it difficult to meet others' expectations of me," and "people expect nothing less than perfection from me." Self-oriented perfectionism involves individually setting exact standards for one to reach as well as strictly evaluating and censuring one's behavior. The SOPS contains fifteen items and includes sample items like, "when I am working on something, I cannot relax until it is perfect" and "I strive to be the best at everything I do." The items were rated on a seven point Likert scale (1 = strongly disagree and 7 = strongly agree). The measures of socially prescribed perfectionism (α = .82) and self-oriented perfectionism (α = .89) were both found to be highly reliable. Hewitt and Flett (1991) found evidence for the discriminant validity of the socially prescribed subscale, since the subscale is not correlated with the self-standard or self-importance measures of the MPS and is significantly related to social behaviors like the fear of negative social evaluation and a need for approval from others.

Perfectionistic self-presentation. The Perfectionistic Self-Presentation Scale (PSPS) was used to assess participants' perfectionistic self-presentation (Hewitt et al., 2003). The PSPS is used to measure perfectionistic self-presentation with three subscales for perfectionistic self-promotion, non-display of imperfection, and nondisclosure of imperfection. The perfectionistic self-promotion subscale contains 10 items and assesses the need to appear perfect; a sample item reads, "I strive to look perfect to others." The non-display of imperfection subscale contains 10 items and assesses the need to avoid appearing imperfect; a sample item reads, "I would like to appear more competent than I really am." The nondisclosure of imperfection contains seven items and assesses the need to avoid public admission of imperfection; a sample item reads, "I should solve my own problems rather than admit them to others." The items were rated by respondent agreement on a seven point Likert scale (1 = *strongly disagree* and 7 = *strongly agree*). Internal consistency was found for the entire measure (α = .93), perfectionistic self-promotion (.89), non-display of imperfection (α = .83), and nondisclosure of imperfection (α = .81). Hewitt et al. (2003) also demonstrated construct validity, since respondent ratings were uniquely associated only with corresponding subscales for both student and clinical samples. There was additionally evidence for the predictive validity for the perfectionistic self-presentation construct on social anxiety.

Perceived social support. The Multidimensional Scale of Perceived Social Support (MSPSS) was used to assess participants' perceived social support (Zimet, Dahlem, Zimet, & Farley, 1988). The MSPSS measures subjective perceptions of social support adequacy; social support is assessed in four items for each of the three sources: family, friends, and a significant other. Social support is a relationship between at least two individuals which is perceived by the recipient as enhancing their well-being (Brownell & Shumaker, 1984; Lin, 1986). Sample items for social support of friends read: "I can talk about my problems with my friends;" sample items for social support of family read: "my family really tries to help me;" and sample items for social support of significant others read: "there is a special person in my life that cares about my feelings." The items were rated by respondent agreement on a 7-point Likert scale (1 = *strongly disagree* and 7 = *strongly agree*). Reliability was found for the entire measure (α = .91), as well as significant others (α = .96), family (α = .90), and friends (α = .91). The MSPSS demonstrates construct validity, since perceived social support was found to be negatively related to anxiety and depression symptoms reported on the Depression and Anxiety subscales of the Hopkins Symptom Checklist (Derogatis, Lipman, Rickels, Uhlenhuth, & Covi, 1974).

Social anxiety. The Social Interaction Anxiety Scale (SIAS) was used to assess participants' social anxiety (Mattick & Clarke, 1998). The SIAS is a 20-item scale used to measure prevalence and severity of social phobia and social anxiety disorders. Respondents rate their experiences in social situations associated with social anxiety criteria in the fourth edition of the Diagnostic and Statistical Manual of Mental Disorders. Sample items include: "I am nervous mixing with people I don't know well" and "I have difficulty talking with other people." Experiences were rated on a 7-point scale (1 = *strongly disagree* and 7 = *strongly agree*). The measure was found to be highly reliable (α = .92). Mattick and Clarke (1998) found evidence for discriminant validity, since scores were differentiated between social phobia and agoraphobia, between agoraphobia and simple phobia, and between social phobia and normal samples (undergraduates and community samples combined); scores were essentially the same between undergraduate and community samples. There is also evidence of construct validity for the SIAS, since the scale was intercorrelated with other social anxiety scales (Beck & Beck, 1972; Craig & Andrews, 1985; Marks & Mathews, 1979; Spielberger, Gorsuch, & Lushene, 1970; Watson & Friend, 1969).

RESULTS

See Table 1 for mean scores and a correlation matrix of all other study variables.

Bivariate correlational analyses were run to test the first hypothesis that socially prescribed perfectionism would be positively related to social anxiety and perfectionistic self-presentation. Hierarchal regressions were run to test the second hypothesis that perceived social support would moderate the relationship between socially prescribed perfectionism and social anxiety and the relationship between socially prescribed perfectionism and perfectionistic self-presentation. That is, it was expected that perfectionism would be negatively related to social support; social support would be negatively related to social anxiety; social support would be negatively related to perfectionistic self-presentation; and the effects of perfectionism on social anxiety and of perfectionism on perfectionistic self-presentation would be greater among students who perceiving themselves as having low levels of social support.

Consistent with the first hypothesis, socially prescribed perfectionism relates to social anxiety and perfectionistic self-presentation. See Table 1. Socially prescribed perfectionism significantly and positively correlated with social anxiety, $r(129) = .45$, $p = .000$, and perfectionistic self-presentation, $r(129) = .58$, $p = .000$.

Second, it was determined how socially prescribed perfectionism relates to perceived social support. Socially prescribed perfectionism significantly and negatively related to perceived social support, $r(129) = -.42$, $p = .000$.

Third, it was determined how perceived social support relates to social anxiety and perfectionistic self-presentation. Social support was significantly and negatively related to social anxiety, $r(129) = -.39$, $p = .000$, and perfectionistic self-presentation, $r(129) = -.28$, $p = .001$.

Other correlational findings include the significant, positive relationship between socially prescribed perfectionism and self-oriented perfectionism, $r(129) = .46$, $p = .000$. Self-oriented perfectionism was significantly, positively related to perfectionistic self-presentation, $r(129) = .60$, $p = .000$, but unrelated to perceived social support and social anxiety. Perfectionistic self-presentation and social anxiety were also significantly, positively related, $r(129) = .53$, $p = .000$.

In order to examine perceived social support as a moderator on the relationship between socially prescribed

Table 1						
Mean Scores and Correlation Matrix of all the Study Variables						
	Mean	1.	2.	3.	4.	5.
1. Socially Prescribed Perfectionism	3.78	--				
2. Self-Oriented Perfectionism	4.78	.46***	--			
3. Perceived Social Support	5.68	-.42***	.01	--		
4. Social Anxiety	3.99	.45***	.16	-.39***	--	
5. Perfectionistic Self-Presentation (PSP)	4.26	.58***	.60***	-.28**	.53***	--
Note. ** p < .01;*** p < .001.						

Table 2		
Hierarchical Regression Examining Socially Prescribed Perfectionism as a Predictor of Social Anxiety		
	β	R²
Step 1		
Socially Prescribed Perfectionism	.45***	.21***
Step 2		
Socially Prescribed Perfectionism	.35***	.25**
Perceived Social Support	-.24**	
Step 3		
Socially Prescribed Perfectionism	.35***	.26**
Perceived Social Support	-.27**	
Socially Prescribed Perfectionism by Social Support Interaction	.09	
Note. ** p < .01;*** p < .001.		

28

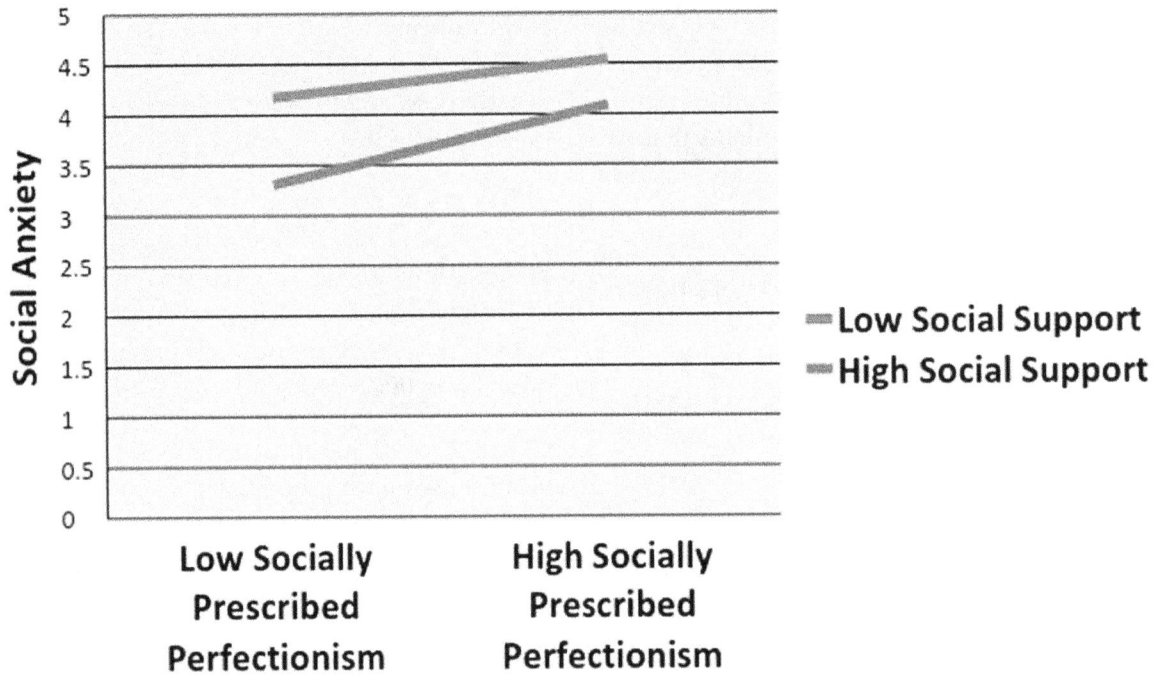

Figure 1. Social Support as a Moderator on the Effect of Socially Prescribed Perfectionism on Social Anxiety

Note: β= .09, p = .249

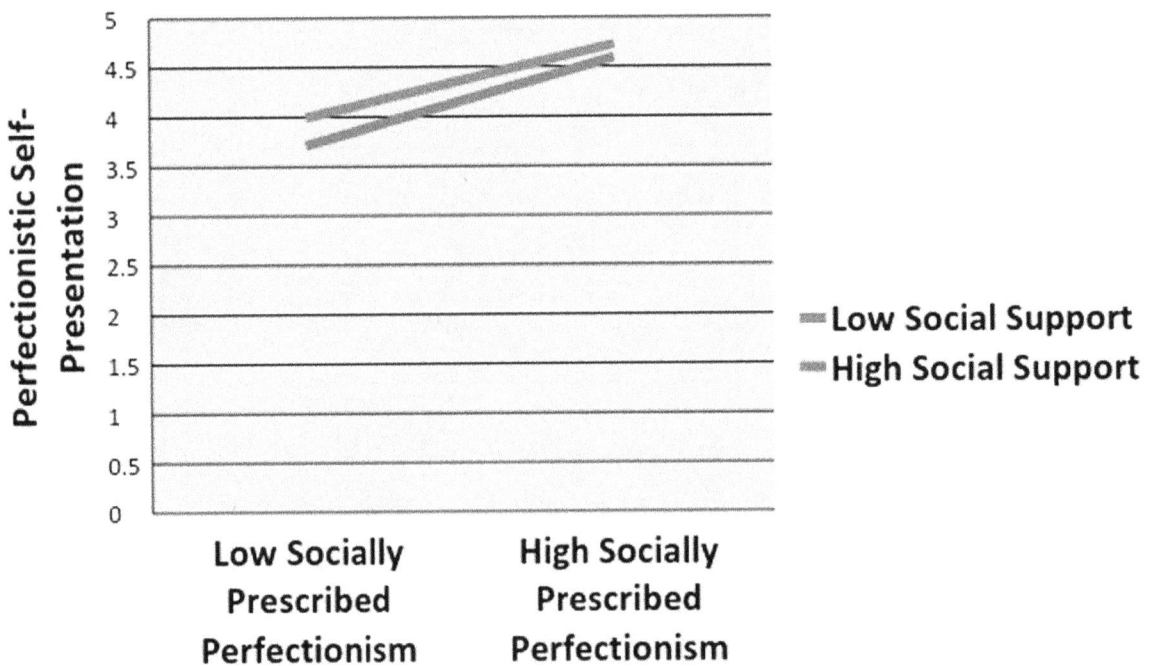

Figure 2. Social Support as a Moderator on the Effect of Socially Prescribed Perfectionism on Perfectionistic Self-Presentation

Note. β= -.07, p = .337

perfectionism and social anxiety and to examine the total effect of socially prescribed perfectionism and the total effect of perceived social support on social anxiety, the data was run through a hierarchal regression analysis. Social anxiety was the dependent variable. Socially prescribed perfectionism was entered on the first step. Perceived social support was inserted on the second step. A socially prescribed perfectionism by perceived social support interaction variable was inserted on the third step of the analysis. See Table 2. On the first step, socially prescribed perfectionism positively related to social anxiety, α (1, 129) = .45, p = .000. Socially prescribed perfectionism accounted for 21 percent of the variance in social anxiety, R^2 = .21, p = .000.

On the second step, there was a direct relationship between socially prescribed perfectionism and social anxiety, α (2, 129) = .35, p = .000. See Table 2. Perceived social support was significantly, negatively related to social anxiety, α (2, 129) = -.24, p = .006. Socially prescribed perfectionism and social support, therefore, were independent main effects of social anxiety, and there were no moderators on the relationship between perfectionism and social anxiety. Perfectionism accounted for 21% of the variance in social anxiety on the first step, and perfectionism and social support accounted for 25% of the variance in social anxiety on the second step. Social support, therefore, accounted for 4% of the variance on social anxiety, R^2 = .25, p = .006. On the third step, the socially prescribed perfectionism by perceived social support interaction variable was not significant predictors of social anxiety. The interaction variable did not explain any additional variance in social anxiety,

R^2 = .26, p = .008, but the total R-square is statistically significant since perfectionism and social support (not the perfectionism by social support interaction) primarily account for the variance in social anxiety. See Figure 1 for a graphical representation of and conceptual support for the interaction model. The graph supports the hypothesis that the effect of perfectionism on social anxiety would be greater among students with low levels of perceived social support, since it illustrates a social support interaction on the association between perfectionism and social anxiety even though the interaction was not statistically significant.

In order to examine perceived social support as a moderator on the relationship between socially prescribed perfectionism and perfectionistic self-presentation and to examine the total effect of socially prescribed perfectionism and the total effect of perceived social support on perfectionistic self-presentation, an additional hierarchical regression analysis was run. The dependent variable for the analysis was perfectionistic self-presentation. Socially prescribed perfectionism was entered on the first step. Perceived social support was entered on the second step. A socially prescribed perfectionism by perceived social support interaction was inserted on the third step. See Table 3. The findings indicate on the first step that socially prescribed perfectionism positively related to perfectionistic self-presentation, α (1, 129) = .58, p = .000. Socially prescribed perfectionism accounted for 33% of the variance in perfectionistic self-presentation, R^2 = .33, p = .000.

On the second step, there was a direct relationship between socially prescribed perfectionism and per-

Table 3			
Hierarchical Regression Examining Socially Prescribed Perfectionism as a Predictor of Perfectionistic Self-Presentation			
		β	R²
Step 1			
	Socially Prescribed Perfectionism	.58***	.33***
Step 2			
	Socially Prescribed Perfectionism	.56***	.34
	Perceived Social Support	-.04	
Step 3			
	Socially Prescribed Perfectionism	.56***	.34
	Perceived Social Support	-.02	
	Socially Prescribed Perfectionism X Perceived Social Support	-.07	
Note. *** p < .001.			

fectionistic self-presentation, α (2, 129) = .56, p = .000. See Table 2. Perceived social support did not have a significant association with perfectionistic self-presentation. Therefore, only socially prescribed perfectionism predicted and was a main effect of perfectionistic self-presentation, and there were no moderators on the relationship between perfectionism and perfectionistic self-presentation. On the third step, the socially prescribed perfectionism by perceived social support interaction was not a significant predictor of perfectionistic self-presentation. See Figure 2 for a graphical representation of the interaction model.

DISCUSSION

The present study examined the role of socially prescribed perfectionism, perfectionistic self-presentation, and social anxiety in college students. I expected that socially prescribed perfectionism would be related to social anxiety and perfectionistic self-presentation behaviors. Moreover, I predicted that social support would influence the relationship between perfectionism and social anxiety and between perfectionism and perfectionistic self-presentation.

The findings were consistent with the first hypothesis that socially prescribed perfectionism would be associated with social anxiety and perfectionistic self-presentation. The findings were conceptually consistent, although mathematically insignificant, with the second hypothesis that socially prescribed perfectionism would have a relationship with social anxiety influenced by levels of college students' perceived social support. The findings were inconsistent with the third hypothesis that the effect of socially prescribed perfectionism on perfectionistic self-presentation would be greater for students with lower levels of social support.

Some notable findings that were not part of any of the hypothesis regard self-oriented perfectionism. While it is clear that socially prescribed perfectionism is related to maladaptive outcomes, like social anxiety and perfectionistic self-presentation behaviors, the adaptability and maladaptibility of self-oriented perfectionism is more unclear. Past research has noted the ambiguity of self-oriented perfectionism. Dunkley et al. (2000) suggest the adaptability of self-oriented perfectionism, while Hewitt and Flett (1991) associate self-oriented perfectionism with the maladaptive form. The findings of the current study indicate that self-oriented perfectionistic tendencies are related to maladaptive perfectionistic impression management behaviors but are unrelated to social anxiety. The present study, thus, suggests that self-oriented perfectionism is related to some maladaptive outcomes but may still generally considered to be less maladaptive than socially prescribed perfectionism.

Consistencies in Previous Perfectionism Studies

The finding that socially prescribed perfectionism is associated with social anxiety and perfectionistic self-presentation in college students is consistent with previous findings in other studies. The correlational findings are consistent with past findings that found direct relationships between social anxiety (Laurenti et al., 2008; Nepon et al., 2011, Saboonchi & Lundh, 1997) and perfectionistic self-presentation (Hewitt et al., 2003; Stoeber & Roche, 2014) with socially prescribed perfectionism in college students. The finding that self-oriented perfection is associated with perfectionistic self-presentation is also consistent with past research. Hewitt and Flett (2003) found that the facets of perfectionistic self-presentation are related to self-oriented perfectionistic tendencies.

Moreover, the conceptual finding that the effect of socially prescribed perfectionism on social anxiety is greater among students with low levels of social support is relatively consistent with previous literature. A recent study found that social support moderates the relationship between perfectionism and anxiety/depression, although the perfectionism measure indicated positive and negative perfectionism (Zhou, et al., 2013). Nevertheless, high levels of social support seem to play a role in reducing anxiety in perfectionists who strive for perfection to please others. Both studies also found such interaction effects in college students. The present study expands the findings of Zhou et al. (2013) and perfectionism literature by including an American sample compared with the previous study's Chinese sample. The current study also investigated how perfectionism and social support relate to social anxiety compared with anxiety and depression with an alternative measure of trait perfection.

Possible Explanations for Unexpected Findings

The finding that there is no greater effect of socially prescribed perfectionism on perfectionistic self-presentation when college students have lower levels of social support is unexpected. While a social support system may influence whether socially prescribed perfectionists are at risk of developing social anxiety, social support does not seem to impact how perfectionists engage in maladaptive presentation behaviors. The findings suggest that students who strive for perfection prescribed by others are likely to engage in perfectionistic self-presentation, whether or not those students perceive themselves as having social support in their lives. That is, students who have a tendency to attain exact standards due to the expectations of others are likely to engage in perfectionistic self-presentation behaviors, like actively promoting their instances of perfection and avoiding discussion and display of imperfection, whether or not they have a social support system of significant others, friends, and family in their lives. A possible explanation for the unexpected finding is that perfectionists may be engaging in these perfectionistic impression management behaviors because the impulse to engage in such behaviors is internally derived from the perfectionist, so social support, an external influencer, would not play a role on the relationship between trait perfectionism and perfectionistic self-presentation. It is also important to consider how the sample includes primarily white, female students, so perhaps social support does not affect whether these particular perfectionistic students will engage in perfectionistic self-presentation.

Limitations and Future Directions

The present study has some limitations. It should be noted that the extreme majority of the sample included mainly white, female underclassmen, so generalizability is limited to those populations. Moreover, the study was non-experimental in design, and the findings do not indicate causal relationships between perfectionism and social anxiety. For example, socially anxious students may develop perfectionistic tendencies in order to compensate in social situations. Although, a longitudinal study found that perfectionistic self-presentation behaviors predict social anxiety in primarily white undergraduate women, which

suggests that students who engage in perfectionistic behaviors are at risk of developing social anxiety (Mackinnon et al., 2014). It must also be considered that although the interaction of social support on the association between socially prescribed perfectionism and social anxiety is conceptually relevant, it is not mathematically significant.

Therefore, future research could replicate the current study with a more diverse sample and with larger sample sizes to increase power for finding statistically significant data. Moreover, future studies could focus on examining perfectionistic students, particularly perfectionists who try to attain exact standards prescribed by others, and the development of social anxiety in a longitudinal design. A longitudinal design could determine whether perfectionists' levels of social support affects whether or not those individuals develop social anxiety. Furthermore, future research can investigate whether certain social networks, such as just friends or significant others, rather than general social support, has a greater influence affecting the association between perfectionism and social anxiety. Additionally, studies could longitudinally observe students who engage in perfectionistic self-presentation impression management behaviors and identify if social support affects the development of social anxiety, since the current study and past research (Mackinnon et al. 2014) have identified as association between perfectionistic self-presentation and social anxiety.

Although future research should address limitations and inconsistent findings, the current study has several findings and implications. The study suggests direct relationships between social anxiety and perfectionistic self-presentation with trait perfectionism. The findings also suggest that self-oriented perfectionism can be quite maladaptive, since it is related to perfectionistic self-presentation, but less maladaptive than socially prescribed perfectionism. The study also suggests conceptual support for the influence of perceived social support on the relationship between socially prescribed perfectionism and social anxiety. Perfectionists who strive for perfection prescribed by others have the potential risk of developing social anxiety when they have low levels of social support and possible reduced risk of developing social anxiety when they have high levels of social support. Future studies should incorporate new samples and longitudinal designs to address inconsistencies and insignifi-cant data and to identify the interaction model of so-cial support on socially prescribed perfectionism and social anxiety. It is necessary and worthwhile to con-tinue research on perfectionism and social anxiety, since knowledge about such relationships can provide clinicians, counselors, educators, parents, and others with awareness about the way in which personality traits, particularly maladaptive traits, influence the development of anxiety disorders. Since over 80% of the sample included first years and sophomores in college, individuals trying to help perfectionistic and socially anxious students should be aware of the vul-nerability of underclassmen, especially freshmen and transfer students, at college and the importance of providing those students with social support.

REFERENCES

Anxiety and Depression Association of America. (2015). *Understanding the facts: Social anxiety disorder*. Retrieved from http://www.adaa.org/understanding-anxiety/social-anxiety-disorder

Beck, A. T., & Beck, R. W. (1972). Screening depressed patients in family practice: A rapid technique. *Postgraduate Medicine, 52*(6), 81-85.

Besser, A., Flett, G. L., & Hewitt, P. L. (2010). Perfectionistic self-presentation and trait perfectionism in social problem-solving ability and depressive symptoms. *Journal of Applied Social Psychology, 40*(8), 2121-2154. doi:10.1111/j.1559-1816.2010.00653.x

Calsyn, R. J., Winter, J. P., & Burger, G. K. (2005). The relationship between social anxiety and social support in adolescents: A test of competing causal models. *Adolescence, 40*(157), 103-113.

Craig, A., & Andrews, G. (1985). The prediction and prevention of relapse in stuttering: The value of self-control techniques and locus of control measures. *Behavior Modification, 9*(4), 427-442. doi:10.1177/01454455850094002

Derogatis, L. R., Lipman, R. S., Rickels, K., Uhlenhuth, E. H., & Covi, L. (1974). The hopkins symptom checklist (HSCL): *A self-report symptom inventory. Behavioral Science, 19*(1), 1-15. doi:10.1002/bs.3830190102

Dunkley, D. M., Blankstein, K. R., Halsall, J., Williams, M., & Winkworth, G. (2000). The relation between perfectionism and distress: Hassles, coping, and perceived social support as mediators and moderators. *Journal of Counseling Psychology, 47*(4), 437-453. doi:10.1037/0022-0167.47.4.437

Dunn, J. C., Whelton, W. J., & Sharpe, D. (2006). Maladaptive perfectionism, hassles, coping, and psychological distress in university professors. *Journal of Counseling Psychology, 53*(4), 511-523. doi:10.1037/0022-0167.53.4.511

Flett, G. L., Druckman, T., Hewitt, P. L., & Wekerle, C. (2012). Perfectionism, coping, social support, and depression in maltreated adolescents. *Journal of Rational-Emotive & Cognitive-Behavior Therapy, 30*(2), 118-131. doi:10.1007/s10942-011-0132-6

Flett, G. L., Endler, N. S., Tassone, C., & Hewitt, P. L. (1994). Perfectionism and components of state and trait anxiety. *Current Psychology, 13*(4), 326-350. doi:10.1007/BF02686891

Frost, R. O., Marten, P., Lahart, C., & Rosenblate, R. (1990). The dimensions of perfectionism [Abstract]. *Cognitive Therapy and Research, 14*(5), 449-468. doi:10.1007/BF01172967

Gnilka, P. B., Ashby, J. S., & Noble, C. M. (2012). Multidimensional perfectionism and anxiety: Differences among individuals with perfectionism and tests of a coping-mediation model. *Journal of Counseling & Development, 90*(4), 427-436. doi:10.1002/j.1556-6676.2012.00054.x

Hewitt, P. L., & Flett, G. L. (1991). Perfectionism in the self and social contexts: Conceptualization, assessment, and association with psychopathology. *Journal of Personality and Social Psychology, 60*(3), 456-470. doi:10.1037/0022-3514.60.3.456

Hewitt, P. L., Flett, G. L., Sherry, S. B., Habke, M., Parkin, M., Lam, R. W.,...Stein, M. B. (2003). The interpersonal expression of perfection: Perfectionistic self-presentation and psychological distress. *Journal of Personality and Social Psychology, 84*(6), 1303-1325. doi:10.1037/0022-3514.84.6.1303

Hewitt, P. L., Flett, G. L., & Weber, C. (1994). Dimensions of perfectionism and suicide ideation. *Cognitive Therapy and Research, 18*(5), 439-460. doi.org:10.1007/BF02357753

Hewitt, P. L., Norton, G. R., Flett, G. L., Callander, L., & Cowan, T. (1998). Dimensions of perfectionism, hopelessness, and attempted suicide in a sample of alcoholics. *Suicide and Life-Threatening Behavior, 28*(4), 395-406. doi:10.1111/j.1943-278X.1998.tb00975.x

Jackson, T., Fritch, A., Nagasaka, T., & Gunderson, J. (2002). Towards explaining the association between shyness and loneliness: A path analysis with American college students. *Social Behavior and Personality, 30*(3), 263-270. doi:10.2224/sbp.2002.30.3.263

Jain, M., & Sudhir, P. M. (2010). Dimensions of perfectionism and perfectionistic self-presentation in social phobia. *Asian Journal of Psychiatry, 3*(4), 216-221. doi:10.1016/j.ajp.2010.08.006

Kim, J. & Lee, J. R. (2011). The Facebook paths to happiness: Effects of the number of Facebook friends and self-presentation on subjective well-being. *Cyberpsychology, Behavior, and Social Networking, 14*(6), 359-364. doi:10.1089/cyber.2010.0374

Kuzel, R. J. (1996). Treating comorbid depression and anxiety. *The Journal of Family Practice, 43*(6), S45-S53.

Laurenti, H. J., Bruch, M. A., & Haase, R. F. (2008). Social anxiety and socially prescribed perfectionism: Unique and interactive relationships with maladaptive appraisal of interpersonal situations. *Personality and Individual Differences, 45*(1), 55-61. doi:10.1016/j.paid.2008.02.018

Li, H., Kou, C., & Gao, Y. (2010). Emotion and social support characteristics of bloggers in a college. *Chinese Mental Health Journal, 24*(10), 801-804.

Lin, N., & Dumin, M. (1986). Access to occupations through social ties. *Social Networks, 8*(4), 365-385. doi:10.1016/0378-8733(86)90003-1

Mackinnon, S. P., Battista, S. R., Sherry, S. B., & Stewart, S. H. (2014). Perfectionistic self-presentation predicts social anxiety using daily diary methods. *Personality and Individual Differences, 56*, 143-148. doi:10.1016/j.paid.2013.08.038

Marks, I. M., & Mathews, A. M. (1979). Brief standard self-rating for phobic patients. *Behaviour Research and Therapy, 17*(3), 263-267. doi:10.1016/0005-7967(79)90041-X

Mattick, R., & Clarke, J. C. (1998). Development and validation of measure of social phobia scrutiny fear and social interaction anxiety. *Behavior Research and Therapy 36*(4), 455-470. doi:10.1016/S0005-7967(97)10031-6

Nepon, T., Flett, G. L., Hewitt, P. L., & Molnar, D. S. (2011). Perfectionism, negative social feedback, and interpersonal rumination in depression and social anxiety. *Canadian Journal of Behavioural Science, 43*(4), 297-308. doi:10.1037/a0025032

Saboonchi, F., & Lundh, L. (1997). Perfectionism, self-consciousness and anxiety. *Personality and Individual Differences, 22*(6), 921-928. doi:10.1016/S0191-8869(96)00274-7

Schlenker, B. R., & Leary, M. R. (1982). Social anxiety and self-presentation: A conceptualization model. *Psychological Bulletin, 92*(3), 641-669. doi:10.1037/0033-2909.92.3.641

Schry, A. R., & White, S. W. (2013). Understanding the relationship between social anxiety and alcohol use in college students: A meta-analysis. *Addictive Behaviors, 38*(11), 2690-2706. doi:10.1016/j.addbeh.2013.06.014

34

Sherry, S. B., Hewitt, P. L., Lee-Baggley, D., Flett, G. L., & Besser, A. (2004). Perfectionism and thoughts about having cosmetic surgery performed. *Journal of Applied Biobehavioral Research, 9*(4), 244-257. doi:10.1111/j.1751-9861.2004.tb00103.x

Sherry, S. B., Law, A., Hewitt, P. L., Flett, G. L., & Besser, A. (2008). Social support as a mediator of the relationship between perfectionism and depression: A preliminary test of the social disconnection model. *Personality and Individual Differences, 45*(5), 339-344. doi:10.1016/j.paid.2008.05.001

Shumaker, S. A., & Brownell, A. (1984). Toward a theory of social support: Closing conceptual gaps. *Journal of Social Issues, 40*(4), 11-36. doi:10.1111/j.1540-4560.1984.tb01105.x

Smith, T. W., Ingram, R. E., & Brehm, S. S. (1983). Social anxiety, anxious self-preoccupation, and recall of self-relevant information. *Journal of Personality and Social Psychology, 44*(6), 1276-1283. doi:10.1037/0022-3514.44.6.1276

Spielberger, C., Gorsuch, A., & Lushene, R. (1970). *State-Trait Anxiety Inventory.* Palo Alto, CA: Consulting Psychologists Press.

Stoeber, J., & Roche, D. L. (2014). Affect intensity contributes to perfectionistic self-presentation in adolescents beyond perfectionism. *Journal of Rational-Emotive & Cognitive-Behavior Therapy, 32*(2), 164-180. doi:10.1007/s10942-013-0176-x

Terry-Short, L. A., Glynn Owens, R., Slade, P. D., & Dewey, M. E. (1995). Positive and negative perfectionism. *Personality and Individual Differences, 18*(5), 663-668. doi:10.1016/0191-8869(94)00192-U

Watson, D., & Friend, R. (1969). Measurement of social-evaluative anxiety. *Journal of Consulting and Clinical Psychology, 33*(4), 448-457. doi:10.1037/h0027806

Watson, P. J., Varnell, S. P., & Morris, R. J. (1999). Self-reported narcissism and perfectionism: An ego-psychological perspective and the continuum hypothesis. *Imagination, Cognition and Personality, 19*(1), 59-69. doi:10.2190/MD51-7P8N-WEYE-9H3X

Wonderlich-Tierney, A. L., & Vander Wal, J. S. (2010). The effects of social support and coping on the relationship between social anxiety and eating disorders. *Eating Behaviors, 11*(2), 85-91. doi:10.1016/j.eatbeh.2009.10.002

Zhang, B., & Cai, T. (2012). Coping styles and self-esteem as mediators of the perfectionism-depression relationship among Chinese undergraduates. *Social Behavior and Personality, 40*(1), 157-168. doi:10.2224/sbp.2012.40.1.157

Zhou, X., Zhu, H., Zhang, B., & Cai, T. (2013). Perceived social support as a moderator of perfectionism, depression, and anxiety in college students. *Social Behavior and Personality, 41*(7), 1141-1152. doi:10.2224/sbp.2013.41.7.1141

Zimet, G. D., Dahlem, N. W., Zimet, S. G., & Farley, G. K. (1988). The multidimensional scale of perceived social support. *Journal of Personality Assessment, 52*(1), 30-41. doi:10.1207/s15327752jpa5201_2

An Interview with Mohammed Hossain

Hometown: *Brooklyn, NY*

Major: *Double major in Philosophy and Psychology*

Hobbies: *Jazz, Lindy Bop dancing/teaching, traveling, dance competitions, listening to uplifting music (classical and jazz), current favorite tv show is Viking.*

Do/did you like Geneseo? Why did you choose to come to Geneseo?

Mohammed: I wanted some kind of independence because I would not have been able to achieve the same level of focus in my household. Students at Geneseo have the opportunity to do what they want in terms of independence, and it is less expensive than other good schools. Here, you can study what you want for less. I also think Geneseo is a good place to discover what you want to do.

Why do you feel that GREAT Day is important?

GREAT Day is one of the only days when students get to be proactive in what they show their peers. In other circumstances, a student might be writing a paper, or doing a presentation for a class. They are mostly encouraged to do work through extrinsic motivation, that being that they get a grade at the end of the semester and do not want to fail their classes because they need a degree to get a job. But GREAT Day is an opportunity for students to showcase exactly what they want because they *want* to do it and for no other reason, which is important.

How did it feel to present your work at GREAT Day?

I really enjoyed presenting. It was the first time I did a presentation out of my own volition instead of using a prescribed assignment as motivation. The subject matter presented in my paper was something that I was really, genuinely, interested in. My thesis was an idea that I generally believe and so even though it was based off of a very impersonal, broad subject, it felt very intimate to me. I was really putting myself out there and telling people what I believed and why I believed that to be case. It was nice to have people chime in and respond to that.

A Critique of Antiphon's Justice through the Lens of Socrates' Position on Nomoi and Phusis

Mohammed Hossain

ABSTRACT

Inquiries on justice, law, and natural order can often incite interesting debate and discussion. Questions such as "what is justice" and "what is the role of law and natural order in relation to justice" are among these inquiries. Although they can have many implications for contemporary issues, these inquiries are certainly not just *modern* problems by any means. In fact, these are fundamental questions about society that have been posed since the days of Plato, Socrates, and pre-Socratic philosophers of Ancient Greece. Antiphon and Plato, in particular, have interesting views on natural order and law, and they both offer opposing perspectives. I will elaborate on both of their arguments about justice with respect to its relationship to the law and natural order, as well as justify my position in support of Plato's view—that Antiphon's justice does not lead to a good life.

In Plato's *Crito,* Antiphon and Socrates provide interesting perspectives on life, justice, and the relationship between laws and members of a society. Both discuss a seemingly opposing relationship between laws that are written to govern a society and the fundamental nature of people who are not inclined to follow these laws. A distinction is drawn between what Antiphon dubs *nomoi* and *phusis.* Nomoi represents laws that are made by individuals of a society in order to establish social order. They are made by mutual agreements between people to set limitations on conduct. Phusis, on the other hand, represents the natural order of the world and how people function naturally. Although Socrates does not explicitly use Antiphon's language, he certainly seems to develop arguments about the nature of people, laws created by individuals, and the criteria for a good and just life. Overall, it is Socrates who provides a better justification for the employment of nomoi in living a good and just life. He posits a better method for allowing members of a society to coexist with each other while discouraging the possibility of acting unjustly and harming one another. Socrates' account provides a more plausible argument for a good life as opposed to merely accounting for a free life with the possibility of acting unjustly. In order to fully explain this conclusion, I will discuss essential qualities of

nomoi and phusis, then discuss arguments provided by both Antiphon and Socrates with regard to the relationship between the two laws.

Fragments from Antiphon's writing suggest that nomoi is fundamentally different from phusis in both origin and application. Nomoi are described as "products of agreement, not of natural growth" and "extra additions," while phusis is juxtaposed as "products of natural growth, not agreement" and "necessary" (Antiphon, 2011, p. 156). In other words, nomoi is a result of conventions and parameters created by individuals, while phusis is intrinsic to the nature of the individuals themselves. In terms of their application, nomoi is treated as "important in the presence of witnesses," while phusis is "treated as important while alone and with no witnesses present" (Antiphon, 2011, p. 155). Under nomoi, individuals are "free from penalty" if crimes are not noticed (if they are noticed then crimes are punishable under the law), while phusis is unaffected by observation. The reason for this is that disputes cannot be easily settled by the law if testimony is not provided by anyone other than the accuser and the accused; hence, the presence of witnesses becomes important in order to make one case more persuasive than another in court. From these competing testimonies, justice is maintained by making punishments and amends accordingly. On the other hand, phusis is unaffected by the presence of witnesses because it functions on the will of an individual alone. According to phusis, people should be able to do what they wish, and if they are truly just then they will not do harm to another individual. The harm is not decided by testimony in court, but rather by the circumstances and will of the individuals involved. This is why it is said that under phusis, people are only harmed "as a result of truth" (Antiphon, 2011, p. 156). The nature of nomoi is to set bonds on phusis. If phusis functions under the utility of life, then nomoi is a restriction on that utility in order to establish social order.

Moreover, Antiphon claims that we live from what is advantageous and die from what is not advantageous, but the advantage of nomoi is simply generated from bonds on phusis—this is perhaps where Antiphon begins to move away from a semantic explanation of nomoi and phusis and shifts towards developing arguments concerning the importance of phusis in living a good and just life. The advantages of nomoi that establish social regularity (namely, creating laws against theft, misdemeanor, violence, etc.) are only possible by limiting the freedom of human nature which often functions contrary to these bonds. A problem arises, however, when assuming that nomoi prevents harms from being inflicted on members of a society. Although it may seem like laws can prevent crime, upon inspection, nomoi does not prevent the cause of harm, but merely provides the possibility of punishment and recourse towards a crime inflicted. As Antiphon (2011) puts it:

> …justice that stems from nomoi is insufficient to aid those who submit. In the first place, it permits the one who suffers to suffer and the wrongdoer to do wrong, and it was not at the time of the wrongdoing able to prevent either the sufferer from suffering or the wrongdoer from doing wrong. And when the case is brought to trial for punishment, there is no special advantage for the one who has suffered and that he is able to exact the penalty. And it is open to the wrongdoer to deny it…. However convincing the accusation is on behalf of the accuser, the

defense can be just as convincing. For victory comes through speech (p. 157).

To illustrate this concept, if a business were to be robbed of its merchandise, nomoi could not stop the crime from actually occurring but merely punish the thief and assist the victim. For this reason, it is argued by Antiphon that nomoi is not truly advantageous; it does not prevent harm or cause benefit. Furthermore, punishment for the criminal and recourse for the victim are not guaranteed. They are largely dependent on the persuasiveness of arguments presented in court and not the truth. In this sense, it may be reasonable to see how nomoi fails to bring a good and just life to anyone in a society.

Socrates offers a very different view than Antiphon on nomoi and phusis, starting with a disagreement on Antiphon's notion of an advantageous life. As stated before, Antiphon asserts that phusis should be preferred over nomoi due to the fact that nomoi does not give one an advantageous life and phusis gives one access to the full utility of one's life. In direct opposition Plato's (2002) character Socrates states that the "…important thing is not life, but the good life" (p. 48). This statement implies that a good life is one in which individuals do not harm each other because "doing people harm is no different from wrongdoing" (Plato, 2002, p. 49). In other words, living a good life is distinct from merely living life as a utility, and the distinction stems from the unwillingness of an individual to harm others. This starting point is crucial for understanding why Socrates provides a better justification for the employment of nomoi in living a good and just life. By breaking bonds made with nomoi, an individual cannot live a just life because he is doing harm to the city itself. As Socrates puts it, a city can be destroyed if "…its courts have no force" and if laws are "…nullified and set at naught by private individuals" (Plato, 2002, p. 50). Societies can be destroyed if individuals choose to ignore nomoi and purely follow phusis, which is not just or good in any way. Furthermore, Socrates may disagree with Antiphon's belief that there are no advantages to a life led by nomoi. He cites numerous examples of advantages that Athens had provided him, such as the marriage of his parents leading to his birth and his education. Socrates states: "It is impious to bring violence to bear against your mother or father; it is much more so to use it against your country," implying that every person has a duty to the well-being of their state, and any actions that prove contrary would be impious, harmful, and ultimately unjust as well (Plato, 2002, p. 51). Finally, he answers Antiphon's argument concerning nomoi "binding" phusis by stating these duties one has (to their state) do not bind or enslave people because they have the option to either leave the state (through exile) or accept its terms.

In sum, Socrates provides a more plausible account of living a good and just life by first arguing that a good life is more important than living one free of nomoi and then demonstrating how nomoi fulfills the necessary criteria for providing one with a good life, while phusis lacks in this respect. Antiphon's notion of justice is one in which phusis is used to live one's life to its fullest utility, but taking Socrates' account of justice may prove this idea to be problematic. Antiphon's notion of justice does not practically prevent individuals in a society from inflicting harm upon each other; full utility of one's actions implies possessing the autonomy to do harm. This is not justice, at least when considering Socrates' notion of goodness. In order to promote a good and just life, there must be parameters established in order to prevent people from harming each other. Perhaps one could argue that locking up all the citizens of a society in isolated jail cells would prevent harm, but paradoxically, this is would be very far from a just society. The next best option, then, is to set rules and limitations on the population, which may be enforced through a series of punishments used to discourage socially unacceptable actions through nomoi. The key notion that Antiphon seems to skim over in his criticism of nomoi is the utility of the laws to act as a practical deterrent of harmful actions. This can be seen as Socrates' answer to Antiphon's major criticism of nomoi (that it does not prevent harm but only punishes after the fact, resulting in no advantage): that it should not only serve as a guideline delivering judgments in court, but also guide our daily actions in order to have everyone within a state function accordingly. The result advances the good of everyone in the state as a whole, which is ultimately how a just state and its individuals should function.

For argument's sake, let us suppose that Antiphon may have considered that laws act as a deterrent. Given his previous position in support of phusis, perhaps he would argue that some people have a natural inclination to break laws because they are contrary by their nature, and therefore, adopting civility on the basis of phusis might be more desirable. I believe that an answer to this issue may simply be that Socrates knew this to be true at times and supported nomoi for this very reason. If people naturally possess an inclination to act contrarily to the benefit of a state as a whole, then their actions must be limited in order to ensure that harm is not done. Such an objection would not be problematic for Socrates' support of nomoi. In fact, nomoi can be seen as more meaningful because of the very reason that it acts to limit natural ways in which people may harm each other. Another possible objection to Socrates' position may be that if nomoi is sometimes unjust, then obedience to laws becomes unjust. One would then be required to act unjustly if obeying the laws of a state, and would be punished for acting justly in defiance of the law. An example illustrating this argument may ironically be Socrates' unjust conviction. My answer to such a scenario would simply be that nomoi is not necessarily a static set of rules, but can change and adapt to circumstances based upon the will of members of the society that establish laws; therefore, such unjust nomoi would eventually change to become just. For example, if an individual was convicted of a crime under an unjust law, nomoi would dictate that this individual would be sent to a court to be judged by members of the society (the judge, jury, etc.). If a compelling argument is made that the law does not represent the values of a good and just society, then the court could plausibly rule to change the laws itself and free the convicted man. Practical examples of this would be many Supreme Court decisions (such as *Brown v. Board of Education* and *Plessy v. Ferguson*), which have been used to overrule previous laws that were unjust. In sum, the dynamic nature of nomoi would mean that unjust laws would eventually come to change.

Considering the situation that Socrates was in (being sent to his death due to a false conviction), it would have been understandable for him to agree with Antiphon. After all, if justice had functioned flawlessly under nomoi, he would not have been charged with impiety or corrupting the youth. Nonetheless, Socrates fulfilled his duty as a citizen of Athens by refusing to run away and drinking the hemlock tea. Perhaps Socrates realized that although justice is often difficult to define, we should not be hasty to assume that there is something fundamentally problematic with the idea of agreed limitations on conduct, especially if it is advantageous for the whole of a society. Instead, we should work to have truth reveal itself through discussion and argumentation in court, just as many philosophers do through dialogue and academic disagreement.

REFERENCES

Antiphon. (2011). Antiphon (R. D. McKirahan & P. Curd, Trans.). In P. Curd (Ed.), *A presocratic reader: Selected fragments and testemonia* (2nd ed., pp. 155-160). Indianapolis, IN: Hackett Publishing Company, Inc.

Plato. (2002). Crito (G. M. A. Grube, Trans.). In J. M. Cooper (Ed.), *Plato: Five dialogues* (2nd ed., pp. 45-57). Indianapolis, IN: Hackett Publishing Company, Inc.

An Interview with Leyna Johnson

Hometown: *Spencerport, NY*

Major: *Psychology*

Hobbies: *Reading, sewing, board games.*

Do/did you like Geneseo? Why did you choose to come to Geneseo?

Leyna: A professor I had previously at Monroe Community College told me that Geneseo has the best psychology program in the SUNY system. I knew then that it would be the school I wanted to attend. Especially because I feel I perform better academically in smaller settings.

Geneseo was great, everything from the atmosphere of the town to the friendliness of the staff and student body. Like my previous MCC professor said, I got a really rigorous education that will help me as I pursue higher education.

Why do you feel that GREAT Day is important?

GREAT Day is a great (pardon the pun) opportunity for students. Students are able to showcase what they have been diligently working on, and they can also learn what their friends and classmates have been working on.

How did it feel to present your work at GREAT Day?

Unfortunately, there was a sudden death in my family and I was not able to actually present at GREAT Day because I was out of town. But, I thoroughly enjoyed the process; eagerly awaiting the decision, the elation when picked, the renewed excitement in my own work as I broke my paper down into presentation format, and finally when I returned to town to see that my paper excerpt had still been in the GREAT Day brochure. Although I did not get the full experience, I count myself lucky to have participated in the process.

Are Gender Differences in Bystander Intent to Help a Potential Victim of Party Rape Mediated By Barriers to Help, Rape Myth Acceptance, or Both?

Leyna Johnson

ABSTRACT

This study investigates the individual differences in bystander intent to help a potential victim of party rape. The potential victim was described as an intoxicated woman who was escorted by an apparently sober man into a back bedroom. Undergraduate students at a small liberal arts college (N = 209, 76.1% women) read the description and responded to measures of intent to help, barriers to helping, and rape myth acceptance. As expected, intent to help correlated negatively with barriers to helping and rape myth acceptance. Also as expected, men reported less intent to help, perceived more barriers to helping, and accepted more rape myths than women. Multivariate analyses showed that the gender difference n intent to help was mediated by barriers to helping but not rape myth acceptance. Bystander education programs that explicitly address barriers to helping, including skills deficits and audience inhibition, may be more effective in engaging bystanders to prevent sexual assault.

Campus sexual assault is a common problem in the United States. Krebs, Lindquist, Warner, Fischer, and Martin (2007) found that 19% of college women experience completed or attempted sexual assault; cases define sexual assault as forced touching of a sexual nature, oral sex, sexual intercourse, anal sex, and/or sexual penetration with a finger or object. Party rape is a form of sexual assault that takes place either on or off campus; it typically involves plying the victim with alcoholic beverages to obtain sexual access (Armstrong, Hamilton, & Sweeney, 2006). Twenty percent of college women experience rape, and 72% of the rapes that occurred were attributed to alcohol intoxication (Mohler-Kuo, Dowdall, Koss, & Wechsler, 2004). A common occurrence on college campuses are pre-assault risks. Pre-assault risks are factors that can contribute to an increased likelihood of being a victim of sexual assault. These factors include being female and alone at a party, being female and with friends (male or female) at a party, intoxication of victim or perpetrator, being in a secluded or dark area, and males exhibiting "pre-rape behaviors" (Rozee & Koss, 2001, p. 299).

Pre-rape behaviors include attitudes of sexual entitlement, exhibition of power and control, hostility, anger, and acceptance of interpersonal violence (Rozee & Koss, 2001).

Currently, campus sexual assault is being addressed by bystander educational programs that aim to prevent party rape and other forms of rape. A bystander is a witness to an emergency, crime, or other dangerous situations, but is not directly involved like a victim or perpetrator (Banyard & Moynihan, 2011). Bystander education is the approach to preventing campus sexual assault. By letting the community attempt to intervene and prevent situations within which a party rape might occur, the focus away from victims and perpetrators and encourages individuals in the community to take action (McMahon, 2010). The reduction of bystander inhibition is a major goal of bystander education programs.

Bystander inhibition can be experienced in multiple ways and at various stages of risk awareness. Intervention barriers are internal thoughts or beliefs that prevent a bystander from taking action to prevent party rape. Latané and Darley outlined five steps that need to be taken for a bystander to intervene (as cited in Burn, 2009). Each step has a separate but related barrier; the first step is to notice the event, the second step is to identify the event as intervention-appropriate, the third step is to take responsibility, the fourth step is to decide how to help, and the fifth step is to act to intervene. Burn (2009) found that individuals who experienced greater barriers to helping offered less help in situations of possible party rape within a hypothetical survey. In another hypothetical survey by Bennett, Banyard, and Garnhart (2014), failure to take responsibility and inadequate skills were the most prevalent barriers tied to sexual assault situations. It may be expected that bystanders who experience more barriers will help to female victims of party rape.

Although many situational factors have potential to influence barriers in bystander-helping behavior, personal attitudes on the part of the bystander could also inhibit the act of helping. Rape myths are defined as a complex set of cultural beliefs that lead to the perpetuation of male sexual violence against women (Payne, Lonsway, & Fitzgerald, 1999). Rape myths can affect the perspective of potential bystanders with regard to possibly risky situations, which can in turn affect bystander helping behavior. In a survey of attitudes towards sexual assault, McMahon (2010) found that individuals who accept rape myths more readily were less likely to intervene in potential rape situations than individuals with lower acceptance of rape myths. It may be expected that bystanders with higher rates of rape myth acceptance are less likely than bystanders with lower rates of rape myth acceptance to offer help to female victims of party rape.

Bystander inhibition may be affected by the social group of the victim in relation to the bystander. Social categorization theory suggests that individuals view others in their social group (in-group) more favorably than those outside their social group (out-group). Although social groups tend to have negative associations such as diffusion of responsibility, there are also positive associations such as; social cohesion and co-operation (Turner, Hogg, Oakes, Reicher, & Wetherell, 1987). Consequently, maintaining a positive view of in group members could create a sense of duty in bystanders and influence them to intervene,

an act which would lower bystander inhibition rates. The Levine, Cassidy, Brazier, and Reicher (2002) study was an analogue study in which participants watched a video of a man being attacked. The participants were asked whether or not they would provide help to the man in question; fellow student participants in the same social category were more likely to offer help than participants who were not in the same social category.

Gender is a type of social group. Women may be less likely than men to participate in bystander inhibition and therefore more likely to offer help to a female student at risk for party rape due to their shared gender group. There are mixed results in the literature. The Banyard and Moynihan (2011) study was a retrospective study in which participants were asked about sexual assault in general; women bystanders were found to offer more help than men bystanders. In a longitudinal study of sexual assault attitudes, Banyard (2008) found that women were more likely than men to offer help in situations of sexual assault. However, in an analogue study conducted by Fischer, Greitemeyer, Pollozek, and Frey (2006), participants witnessed a woman being harassed by a physically threatening male or a non-physically threatening male and no gender difference in helping behavior was found. Another analogue study conducted by Levine et al. (2002) found no gender differences in bystander-helping behavior. The lack of gender difference in these two studies may be due to the fact that the studies were based upon physical assault rather than sexual assault.

Some research suggests that men would rather appear to be masculine to other men and the fear of appearing weak is be the reason that men are less likely to help women in rape situations. (Carlson, 2008). An analogue study conducted by Tice and Baumeister (1985) found that when participants heard a potential choking victim, masculine individuals offered less help than other participants. In a hypothetical study where students in an introductory psychology class were asked to answer questions on sexual assault prevention attitudes, opinions, and behaviors, Burn (2009) found that men experience higher numbers of barriers (other than inhibition due to a skills deficit) as bystanders in a pre-assault stage than women. Men give less concrete intervention strategies than do women (Koelsch, Brown, & Boisen, 2012). Because men experience more inhibitions than women, women's offer of help to female victims should be higher. It may be expected that women bystanders are more likely than men bystanders to offer help to a female at risk for party rape.

However, gender differences in rape myth acceptance have been found more consistently. Eyssel, Bohner, and Siebler (2006) found that men who believe they're in a group that has higher rates of rape myth acceptance report higher amounts of rape proclivity. When men perceive their peers as accepting of rape myths, they are more inclined to perpetrate behaviors than intervene. Hinck and Thomas (1999) found that although college students tend to disagree with rape myths in general, men tend to disagree less with rape myths. McMahon (2010) found that men have greater rates of rape myth acceptance than women. A multicultural study found similar results in regards to gender, but determined that American students have higher rape myth acceptance than Scottish students (Muir & Payne, 1996); this difference could be due to American culture promoting higher rape myth acceptance. Further research is needed to understand gender differences in rape myth acceptance, especially in America.

The following study was conducted in order to investigate factors that influence bystander responses to risk for party rape. The first hypothesis stated that bystanders who experience greater barriers to helping will offer less help to victims at risk for party rape. This difference could be due to barriers causing bystander inhibition (Burn, 2009). The second hypothesis was that bystanders who have higher rates of rape myth acceptance will offer less help to victims at risk for party rape. This difference may be due to the acceptance of rape myths inhibiting bystander behavior (McMahon, 2010). The third hypothesis was that men bystanders will experience more barriers than women bystanders, based on research conducted by Burn (2009). The fourth hypothesis was that men bystanders may be more likely than women bystanders to accept rape myths. The fifth hypothesis was that men bystanders might be less likely than women bystanders to offer help to a female at risk for party rape and the sixth hypothesis was that these differences may be due to men experiencing more barriers to helping and accepting more rape myths than women. The current study adds to the literature by building off past retrospective studies on rape myth acceptance and looking at bystander helping behavior offered in an analogue situation (McMahon, 2010). The current study also adds to the limited research on barriers by building off of Burn's (2009) study and by looking at an analogue situation to determine whether bystanders with higher barriers would offer less help.

METHOD

Participants

Data was collected from 209 undergraduates (76.1% female) at a small public college in Western N.Y. The mean age of participants was 19.20 (SD = 1.36), and ranged from 17 to 26. Eighty-five students (40.7%) were freshman, 62 students (29.7%) were sophomores, 41 students (19.6%) were juniors, and 21 students (10.0%) were seniors. One hundred and seventy-two participants (82.3%) responded as White/Caucasian, 14 participants responded as Asian or Asian American (6.7%), 12 participants (5.7%) responded as Black/African American, 10 participants (4.8%) responded as Hispanic/Latino/Chicano, and one participant (0.5%) responded as Native American.

Design

A multivariate correlational design was used within which one between-subjects variable (bystander gender; men and women) was compared to two different sets of dependent variable causes of bystander inhibition (rape myth acceptance and barriers to help) and intent to offer direct help.

Measures

Intent to help. Six bystander helping responses were adapted from Chabot, Tracy, Manning, and Poisson (2009), as well as Levine and Crowther (2008) in the present study. Six direct helping methods (e.g., "ask the drunk girl if she is okay") were assessed to create a scale for direct help. A Likert-type scale was used to determine how likely it was that participants would enact a behavior (1 = *strongly disagree*, 7 = *strongly agree*). Scores were averaged; higher scores indicated greater intent to offer direct help. Reliability of this measure was demonstrated in past research by Katz,

Colbert, and Colangelo (2015). Internal consistency was found to be good in the present study (α = .90).

Barriers to helping. Nine questions with regards to four of the barriers to bystander intervention behavior were adapted from Burn (2009) in the present study. One item from the risk identification barrier was "stay out of it, given no one else seems concerned." Five items were from the failure to take responsibility barrier which was "leave it up to others to get involved." One item from the skills deficit barrier was "know what to say or do in this situation." Two items from the audience inhibition barrier were "worry that if you got involved, you might look stupid" and "decide not to get involved because unsure if others will support you." A Likert-type scale was used to determine how likely it was that participants would experience each barrier (1 = *definitely likely*, 7 = *definitely unlikely*). Scores were averaged and higher scores indicated greater experience of barriers. The author demonstrated the reliability of this measure. In the current study, the estimate of internal consistency was found to be good (α = .85).

Rape myth acceptance. The Illinois Rape Myth Acceptance Short Form (IRMA-SF) was designed to assess participant's agreement with various rape myths and was used in the current study (Payne et al., 1999). The IRMA-SF is composed of 17 items (e.g., "when women are raped, it's often because the way they said "no" was ambiguous"). A Likert-type scale was used to determine how likely participants were to accept rape myths (1 = *strongly disagree*, 5 = *strongly agree*). Scores were averaged with higher scores indicating greater acceptance of rape myths. The authors provided evidence for the reliability of this measure. Internal consistency in the present study was found to be good (α = .86).

Procedure

From an online database provided by the psychology department studies, undergraduate students participated, voluntarily, in a study that dealt with *Attitudes and Reactions of Different Party Safety Messages and Situations*. All participants provided informed consent. Participants filled out surveys in classrooms on campus. Participants were instructed to imagine that they were at a party where they witnessed an intoxicated woman being led into a private bedroom by a seemingly sober man. Participants answered their reaction to the event as well as some personal characteristics on a self-reported scale. Data collection sessions lasted for no longer than an hour. When participants completed their surveys they placed the papers in a slotted box. Participants received extra credit from class as compensation. Full disclosures were provided.

Results

Overall, participants were somewhat likely to offer direct help to potential victims of party rape (M = 4.95, SD = 1.58, ranging from 1 to 7). Participants experienced a moderate amount of barriers (M = 3.27, SD = 1.21, ranging from 1 to 6.63). Rape myth acceptance was low (M = 1.62, SD = 0.50, ranging from 1 to 3.18).

Hypothesis one was that participants who experienced higher numbers of barriers were less likely to provide direct help to a potential victim of party rape than participants who experienced lower numbers of barriers. A negative correlation was found between the number of barriers experienced and the amount of direct help offered to potential victims in the first hypothesis, r (207) = -.67, p < .001. Similarly, hypothesis two stated that there would be a negative correlation between rape myth acceptance and direct help offered to potential victims, r (206) = -.21, p < .01. Again, the second hypothesis was supported by the study.

Hypothesis three and four stated that there would be bystander gender differences in barriers to help as well as rape myth acceptance. Two independent sample t-tests were conducted to examine gender differences in barriers to helping and rape myth acceptance. There also was a significant between-groups difference in barriers, t (206) = -2.63, p < .009. As expected, men bystanders were significantly more likely to experience barriers (M = 3.66, SD = 1.14) than women bystanders (M = 3.15, SD = 1.21). Hypothesis three was supported. There was a significant, between-groups, difference in rape myth acceptance, t (64.21) = -4.61, p < .001. As expected, men bystanders were more likely to accept rape myths (M = 1.94, SD = 0.60) than women bystanders (M = 1.52, SD = 0.41). The fourth hypothesis was supported.

Regression analyses were conducted to examine whether barriers to helping and rape myth acceptance might account for expected gender differences in helping. In the first regression, the gender of the bystander predicted direct help (β = .15, p <.05); full model F (1, 205) = 4.77, p < .05. This suggested significant gender differences in direct helping behavior, supporting hypothesis 5. In a second regression, barriers to help (β = -.65, p <.001) and rape myth acceptance (β = -.06, ns) were added to the model, F (3, 203) = 54.08, p < .001. The significant β, for barriers to help but not rape myth acceptance, suggests that barriers to help explain gender differences more accurately because bystander gender was no longer a significant predictor in the second model (β = .01, ns). The sixth hypothesis was partially supported.

DISCUSSION

The purpose of this study was to investigate factors that influence bystander helping behavior in order to help prevent potential party rape. As expected, bystanders who reported more barriers and higher rates of rape myth acceptance were less likely to offer direct help to a potential victim at risk for party rape than bystanders with lower numbers of barriers and rates of rape myth acceptance. Also as expected, men reported more barriers and higher rates of rape myth acceptance than women. Finally, as expected, men bystanders were less likely to offer help than women bystanders; this gender difference was found to result from barriers to help rather than rape myth acceptance.

The presented study found that, generally, bystanders who have more barriers offer less help than bystanders who have fewer barriers. This finding was similar to Burn's (2009) research, and expands on this research by looking at barriers experienced by bystanders within an analogue situation of party rape. The present study also found that bystanders who accept higher numbers of rape myths offer less direct help than bystanders who accept fewer rape myths. The current results were similar to McMahon's (2010) older results and builds off this research by looking at situations of party rape instead of sexual assault in general, and by using an analogue design as opposed to a retrospective design.

The present study found that men bystanders experienced more barriers to help than women bystanders. The current findings were, again, similar to findings from Burn (2009). The present study found that men bystanders accept more rape myths than women bystanders. The current findings were similar to past results (Muir & Payne, 1996; McMahon, 2010). The present study replicates past findings of gender differences in barriers to help and rape myth acceptance.

The current study found that men bystanders offer less help to potential victims of party rape than women bystanders. The present findings were similar to Banyard (2008) and Levine and Crowther (2008), but differ from Fischer et al. (2006). The current study extends Banyard's (2008) study of sexual assault attitudes by specifically looking at situations of party rape in an analogue design instead of a longitudinal design. The present paper also builds off Levine and Crowther's (2008) study by looking at female victims of potential party rape, not physical violence. In an unambiguous situation of harassment, Fischer et al.'s (2006) study showed no gender differences in helping behavior, but the current study found that gender differences affect helping behavior in an ambiguous situation of party rape.

The present study found that gender differences in bystander help could be attributed to barriers to helping but not rape myth acceptance. Banyard (2008) found that there are gender differences in bystander helping in situations of sexual assault but no potential explanations were explored. The current study expands on Banyard's (2008) study by exploring possible explanations of gender differences in bystander help. Consistent with Burn (2009), the present study found that the more barriers to help that bystanders were presented with, the less likely they were to offer direct help to potential victims of party rape, and that men bystanders experienced more barriers to help than women bystanders. The present study extended past research by showing that gender differences in barriers to help could account for gender differences in direct helping behavior. In contrast to past research, the current study found that to the degree that bystanders accepted more rape myths, they offered less direct help to potential victims of party rape, and rape myth acceptance was higher in men bystanders than women bystanders. However, rape myth acceptance did not explain the gender differences in bystander help offered to potential victims of party rape beyond the direct effect of barriers. Rape myth acceptance could be related to barriers to helping, as shown by a secondary analysis, $r (206) = .22$, $p < .001$, which suggests that rape myth acceptance may affect barriers, and barriers, in turn, explain gender differences in helping behavior. The current study does not explain gender differences in helping as they pertain to rape myth acceptance beyond barriers to help.

Despite the significant findings of the current study, there were limitations. Some limitations to the current study involved participant variability (or lack of), only female victims being represented, and only two possible explanatory factors of bystander inhibition. Most of the participants in the present study were women, and the underrepresentation of men could misrepresent the actual helping behavior in the general population. Multiple studies have found no gender differences in helping behavior (Fischer et al., 2006; Banyard & Moynihan, 2011). Participants predominantly identified as Caucasian in the present study. Although it has been found that party rape is a problem typically associated with individuals who identify as white (Armstrong et al., 2006), having the perspective of a more well-rounded sample might generalize better. The present study only looked at the differences of gender, barriers to help, and rape myth acceptance, when other possible sources of bystander inhibition exist, such as victim blame or empathy, and social status of the victim in relation to the bystander.

The current study found that gender differences in helping behavior could be attributed to barriers to help. However, due to the design of the study, the first barrier, "notice the event," could not be tested. An analogue study could be conducted to include this barrier in testing in order to see whether that specific barrier also has gender differences. Bennett et al. (2014) found that if participants were to notice an event as a pre-assault risk, they would be more likely to intervene. The present study found that overall rape myth acceptance was low and did not contribute to gender differences in bystander helping behavior, but could be linked to barriers to help. Further research could be conducted to examine this link and the role it plays in bystander intervention. For example, a correlational study could be conducted to see

which barriers are affected by rape myth acceptance. Other factors of bystander helping behavior should be researched. For example, do bystanders offer more or less help based on the race or age of the victim? When does a potentially ambiguous situation like the pre-assault risk condition become less ambiguous to potential bystanders? Researchers should focus on which situations promote bystander helping behavior in party rape situations. The current study as well as many past studies (Bennett et al., 2014; Levine et al., 2002) have looked at the relationship between the bystander and the victim in helping behavior. Burn (2009) found that men were likely to intervene when the perpetrator was a friend, but the research did not look at women bystander intervention with perpetrators. Further research can lead to the founding of better bystander education programs which, in turn, could lead to more intervention on behalf of individuals at risk for party rape within the community.

The present study has wide-reaching applications. Krebs et al. (2007) found that one in five college women are victims of sexual assault or attempted sexual assault. The current approach to preventing these crimes is the establishment of bystander intervention programs on college campuses. The current study explores some possible explanations that can be attributed to bystander helping behavior. Further research is necessary to fully understand situations that lead to bystander helping behavior.

REFERENCES

Armstrong, E. A., Hamilton, L., & Sweeney, B. (2006). Sexual assault on campus: A multilevel, integrative approach to party rape. *Social Problems, 53*(4), 483-499. doi:10.1525/sp.2006.53.4.483

Banyard, V. L. (2008). Measurement and correlates of prosocial bystander behavior: The case of interpersonal violence. *Violence and Victims, 23*(1), 83-97. doi:10.1891/0886-6708.23.1.83

Banyard, V. L., & Moynihan, M. M. (2011). Variation in bystander behavior related to sexual and intimate partner violence prevention: Correlates in a sample of college students. *Psychology of Violence, 1*(4), 287-301. doi:10.1037/a0023544

Bennett. S., Banyard, V. M., & Garnhart, L. (2014). To act or not to act, that is the question? Barriers and facilitators of bystander intervention. *Journal of Interpersonal Violence, 29*(3), 476-496. doi:10.1177/0886260513505210

Burn, S. M. (2009). A situational model of sexual assault prevention through bystander intervention. *Sex Roles, 60,* 779-792. doi:10.1007/s11199-008-9581-5

Carlson, M. (2008). I'd rather go along and be considered a man: Masculinity and bystander intervention. *The Journal of Men's Studies, 16*(1), 3-17. doi:10.3149/jms.1601.3

Chabot, H. F., Tracy, T. L., Manning, C. A., & Poisson, C. A. (2009). Sex, attribution, and severity influence intervention decisions of informal helpers in domestic violence. *Interpersonal Violence, 24*(10), 1696-1713. doi:10.1177/0886260509331514

Eyssel, F., Bohner, G., & Siebler, F. (2006). Perceived rape myth acceptance of others predicts rape proclivity: Social norm or judgmental anchoring? *Swiss Journal of Psychology/Schweizerische Zeitschrift Für Psychologie/Revue Suisse De Psychologie, 65*(2), 93-99. doi:10.1024/1421-0185.65.2.93

Fischer, P., Greitemeyer, T., Pollozek, F., & Frey, D. (2006). The unresponsive bystander: Are bystanders more responsive in dangerous emergencies? *European Journal of Social Psychology, 36*(2), 267-278. doi:10.1002/ejsp.297

Hinck, S. S., & Thomas, R. W. (1999). Rape myth acceptance in college students: How far have we come? *Sex Roles, 40*(9), 815-832.

Katz, J., Colbert, S., & Colangelo, L. (2015). Effects of group status and victim sex on female bystanders' responses to a potential party rape. *Violence and Victims, 30*(2), 265-278. doi:10.1891/0886-6708.VV-D-13-00099

Koelsch, L. E., Brown, A. L., & Boisen, L. (2012). Bystander perceptions: Implications for university sexual assault prevention programs. *Violence and Victims, 27*(4), 563-79. doi:10.1891/0886-6708.27.4.563

Krebs, C. P., Lindquist, C. H., Warner, T. D., Fisher, B. S., & Martin, S. L. (2007). *The campus sexual assault (CSA) study: Final Report.* Retrieved from https://www.ncjrs.gov/pdffiles1/nij/grants/221153.pdf

Latane, B., & Darley, J. M. (1970). *The unresponsive bystander: Why doesn't he help?* New York, NY: Appleton-Century-Crofts.

Levine, M., Cassidy, C., Brazier, G., & Reicher, S. (2002). Self-categorization and bystander non-intervention. *Journal of Applied Social Psychology, 32*(7), 1452-1463. doi:10.1111/j.1559-1816.2002.tb01446.x

Levine, M., & Crowther, S. (2008). The responsive bystander: How social group membership and group size encourage as well as inhibit bystander intervention. *Journal of Personality and Social Psychology, 95*(6), 1429-1439. doi:10.1037/a0012634

McMahon, S. (2010). Rape myth beliefs and bystander attitudes among incoming college students. *Journal of American College Health, 59*(1), 3-11. doi:10.1080/07448481.2010.483715

Mohler-Kuo, M., Dowdall, G. W., Koss, M. P., & Wechsler, H. (2004). Correlates of rape while intoxicated in a national sample of college women. *Journal of Studies on Alcohol, 65*(1), 37-45. doi:10.15288/jsa.2004.65.37

Muir, G., Lonsway, K. A., & Payne, D. L. (1996). Rape myth acceptance among Scottish and American students. *The Journal of Social Psychology, 136*(2), 261-262. doi:10.1080/00224545.1996.9714002

Payne, D. L., Lonsway, K. A., & Fitzgerald, L. F. (1999). Rape myth acceptance: Exploration of its structure and its measurement using the Illinois rape myth acceptance scale. *Journal of Research in Personality, 33*(1), 27-68. doi:10.1006/jrpe.1998.2238

Rozee, P. D., & Koss, M. P. (2001). Rape: A century of resistance. *Psychology of Women Quarterly, 25*(4), 295-311. doi:10.1111/1471-6402.00030

Tice, D. M., & Baumeister, R. F. (1985). Masculinity inhibits helping in emergencies: Personality does predict the bystander effect. *Journal of Personality and Social Psychology, 49*(2), 420-428. doi:10.1037/0022-3514.49.2.420

Turner, J. C., Hogg, M. A., Oakes, P. J., Reicher, S. D., & Wetherell, M. S. (1987). A self-categorization theory. *Rediscovering the social group: A self-categorization theory* (pp. 42-67). Oxford, UK: Basil Blackwell Ltd.

An Interview with Cortney Linnecke

Hometown: *Chautauqua Lake, NY*

Major: *Double major in English-Creative Writing and International Relations-Developing Worlds*

Hobbies: *Geneseo Women's Club Hockey Team, Newman Campus Ministries, Gestures: Organization for Deaf Awareness.*

Do/did you like Geneseo? Why did you choose to come to Geneseo?

Cortney: In terms of value, I thought Geneseo offered the highest standard of education at the most affordable cost. Geneseo also offered a wide array of majors and minors (I came in undecided) and a robust study abroad program, both of which were extremely important factors in my decision. I think Geneseo was an important stepping stone for me in terms of transitioning from a small town into the greater world beyond. Not only did Geneseo help broaden my mind regarding my understanding of others, but it also helped me grow as an individual and gain a sense of self-awareness that I did not have before. On top of that, I met some of my very best friends at Geneseo, for which I will always be grateful.

Why do you feel that GREAT Day is important ?

I think GREAT Day is important because it encourages students to go beyond the required coursework in the classroom to pursue knowledge in a way that perhaps feels more personal, creative, and meaningful. GREAT Day was important for me because it allowed me the chance to delve deeply into a topic I really cared about, an obscure topic that I would not have had the chance to explore within the confines of my normal class curriculums.

How did it feel to present your work at GREAT day?

I was nervous to present my work, but it ended up being the best part of the whole experience! After putting so much work into my thesis, it was incredibly rewarding to share my knowledge and passion about conflict in the Congo with other people in a live, immediate setting. Best of all was seeing the audience's interest in my topic and hearing their dialogue after my presentation—raising awareness and instigating conversation about the Congo was my project goal from the very start.

Evaluating Conflict Mineral Legislation in the Democratic Republic of Congo

Cortney Linnecke

INTRODUCTION

Conflict minerals are everywhere. Gold, tin, tantalum, and tungsten can be found in electronics, automobiles, and even jewelry, thus developing an immediate but invisible presence in the lives of consumers. They illustrate a direct relationship between Western consumers and mines in the Democratic Republic of Congo (DRC), and thus a connection between Westerners and miners in the DRC who may operate under conditions of abuse, corruption, and conflict. This presence is described as "invisible" because despite the irrefutable presence of conflict minerals in everyday goods, many consumers remain ignorant of their own connections to a crisis occurring halfway around the world.

In recent years, however, the visibility of conflict in the Congo increased, and along with it conflict minerals began garnering attention. Global leaders started to take notice of the humanitarian abuses occurring in the DRC: mass murder, rape, torture, and ethnic violence. They began drawing connections between the armed groups that committed these abuses, the mines they were fighting to control, and, by extension, connections with multinational companies that were supporting mines and armed groups through the trade of conflict minerals.

Knowledge of the conflict mineral trade elicited different responses from different nations. Some countries, particularly Eastern and Asian countries, decided to separate business interests from humanitarian concerns, and continued investing and trading in the DRC. Other countries, the United States in particular, decided to pass legislation that would prevent multinational corporations from purchasing minerals that had been sourced under conditions of conflict in the DRC.

Specifically, the United States passed the Dodd-Frank Wall Street Reform and Consumer Protection Act (Dodd-Frank Act). Section 1502 of this Act, a small section accounting for only about five pages out of a document 848 pages long, seeks to regulate the relationship between international companies and conflict minerals. It necessitates due diligence, meaning that companies by law must account for the legitimacy and conflict-free nature of any minerals they purchase and use to produce goods. Though the methods to confirm mineral legitimacy may vary, the Dodd-Frank Act is firm in the stance that companies must take measures to source their minerals. They do this by undergoing a series of audits and submitting a series of reports to legitimize their sourcing measures. Similar due diligence laws have been passed by other countries, and the Organization for Economic Co-operation and Development has developed an international framework for the regulation and trade of conflict minerals.

These types of international response were born out of a belief that stopping the purchase of conflict minerals would stop the flow of profits to armed groups in the DRC; that eliminating their income would disband the groups, and that disbanding the armed groups would stop the conflict. While anti-conflict mineral legislation did, in fact, reduce revenues to armed groups in the DRC, it did not disband militaries or terminate the country's conflict. Instead, international companies—turned off by the new costs that accompanied due diligence—began halting investment and trade in the Congo. As a result, the DRC started experiencing newfound plights: local economies collapsed, healthcare declined, children began dropping out of school, and unemployment swelled.

The international response, therefore, produced a paradox. Global leaders had passed laws in an effort to help raise the Congo from its crisis, but in some ways these laws had only aggravated the problem. How could well-intentioned legislation go so horribly awry in execution? Why did no one foresee the negative fall-out of anti-conflict mineral legislation? And perhaps most importantly, what can the global community learn from the failure of anti-conflict mineral legislation and specifically from the failure of the Dodd-Frank Act?

This paper will seek to explore the weaknesses and failings of such legislation in order to propose improvements for the ways in which the global community interacts with and intervenes in the Congo. In order to do this, however, this paper must start at the beginning. The story of anti-conflict mineral legislation does not start in 2010 with the Dodd-Frank Act. Rather, this paper must take into account the history of the Congo, the actualities of mining, production and trade in the DRC, and the specifics of the legislation itself. All of these are necessary components in attaining a thorough understanding of how and why anti-conflict mineral legislation failed in the ways that it did. This, in turn, is important because it is only through understanding the failures of anti-conflict mineral legislation that the global community can begin to craft realistic solutions for peace.

BACKGROUND

The DRC's relations with Europe began in 1482, when Diogo Cao—a Portuguese explorer—first visited the country (Democratic Republic of Congo Profile, 2015). Cao established ties with the monarchy of the Kongo empire, which had come to power roughly two centuries earlier in the 1200s (Democratic Republic of Congo Profile, 2015).

However, it wasn't until the 16th and 17th centuries that European interest in the Congo really gained momentum. During this time, slave traders from Portugal, France, Great Britain, and the Netherlands exported roughly one million Africans from the Loango Coast (Democratic Republic of Congo Profile, 2015). Other statistics are less modest in their estimation of slaves sold in this timeframe, placing the numbers closer to 3 million and 13 million (Haskin, 2005). No matter the exact number of lives trafficked, the slave trade, which flourished until the 1830s, had lasting impacts on the Congolese way of life. It disrupted existing social hierarchies, encouraged a view of humanity that devalued individuals as expendable commodities, and imported foreign goods and ideas such as alcohol, guns, and the seeds of capitalism (Gondola, 2005).

Perhaps more than anything, however, the slave trade opened the door for European imperialism and the subsequent colonization of the Congo. With the advent of the Industrial Revolution in Europe, demand for the natural resources of Africa—such as rubber, ivory, palm oil, lumber, and peanuts—dramatically increased. Since the far-reaching effects of the slave trade had weakened Africa, the people of the Congo were therefore rendered essentially incapable of withstanding Europe's invasion (Gondola, 2005).

In 1885, King Leopold II of Belgium established the Congo Free State, which would become an official colony of Belgium in 1908 (Democratic Republic of Congo Profile, 2015). The realities of Leopold's rule were harsh and barbaric. He plundered the Congo's natural resources and committed many serious human rights violations through his extractive efforts (Arieff, 2014). These abuses included taking women and children hostage to ensure men's cooperation in forced labor, as well as imposing brutal punishments on any Congolese who failed to meet extraction quotas or pay the taxes that were levied to ludicrous rates under his rule (Haskin, 2005). Punishments were inflicted in varying shades of brutality along a spectrum of violence: chopping off hands and ears, floggings with a *chicotte* (a sharp, spiked hide), being shot, being hanged, and being beheaded (Haskin, 2005). The exact number of casualties incurred under Leopold's reign remains uncertain, but estimates range anywhere from 5 million to 22 million deaths (Haskin, 2005). With such methods, Leopold set an example of authority that derived its power from brute force and violence, initiating an unfortunate pattern of turbulence to come among Congolese leaders.

But Leopold's damage was not limited solely to the destruction of lives. He also reinforced ethnic divides by mandating that the Congolese list a tribal identity when completing governmental forms, which "tended unconsciously to breed ethnic awareness" (Young, 1965, p. 266). Such awareness would resurface as ethnic tension and conflict years later. Along with the Catholic Church, Leopold also laid a foundation of instability in the Congo by repressing the education of its citizens. Education in the Congo Free State extended only to secondary school, although most students did not make it to even that level. This limit on education was imposed in an effort to prevent uprisings and organized resistance to Belgian rule; the Catholic slogan of the time even quipped, "No elite, no problem" (Haskin, 2005, p. 3). While this initiative would not ultimately prevent revolution in the Congo Free State, it would sow ignorance and inexperience among the Congolese in terms of self-rule. Thus, even when the Congolese finally achieved independence, they struggled to re-order the country and achieve effective self-administration (Haskin, 2005).

In 1965, a military colonel named Mobutu Sese Seko seized power (Democratic Republic of Congo Profile, 2015). He would rule for three decades under what has now been described as a "kleptocratic…reign of terror" (Haskin, 2005, p. 6). Mobutu stripped citizens of their fundamental rights, committed atrocities as a means of generating fear, relied on fraudulent elections and corrupt political tactics, and allowed civil conflicts from neighboring countries to spill over the DRC's borders (Haskin, 2005). In particular, Mobutu welcomed Hutu extremists—the perpetrators of the Rwandan genocide of the early 1990s—into Zaire's refugee camps, which upset among Zairian Tutsis, Rwanda's newly established Tutsi government, and Burundi (Arieff, 2014). The tumultuous presence of foreign refugees and military groups is a problem that the DRC still struggles with today.

In 1997, rebel forces assisted by Rwanda, Uganda, and Angola overthrew Mobutu and the more liberal Laurent Kabila came to power (Democratic Republic of Congo Profile, 2015). Under Kabila the DRC saw political upheaval, Africa's first World War, and ultimately the assassination of Kabila himself (Democratic Republic of Congo Profile, 2015). Under Laurent Kabila's rule, an additional 3 million Congolese succumbed to disease, violence, starvation, and other sufferings (Haskin, 2005).

Laurent Kabila was succeeded by his son, Joseph Kabila (Arieff, 2014). Under his reign, the DRC experienced a transitional government period in 2003, received a new constitution in 2005, and underwent their first "relatively free and fair" (Arieff, 2014, p. 120) multiparty elections in 2006. Despite these successes, the DRC today remains a hotbed of conflict, violence, and economic suffering. Additionally, the country continues to maintain complex, strained, and even volatile relations with its neighboring nations of Uganda, Rwanda, and Angola (Arieff, 2014).

It is within these modern and delicate circumstances, and emerged from this history of turbulence, brutality, and strife, that the conversation surrounding the conflict mineral trade is rooted in and built upon today.

MINING, PRODUCTION AND TRADE IN THE DRC

The Context

Mining is the cornerstone of the DRC's economy. Besides mining's social and political implications, it also impacts the nation's gross domestic product, foreign exchange generation, budgetary revenues, and employment statistics (Engineering and Mining Journal, 2000). The Natural Resource Governance Institute (n.d.) estimated that in 2010 the extractive sector accounted for twenty percent of the DRC's gross domestic product. Despite mining's crucial role in the economic life of the DRC, it has been implicated in conflict and has not contributed to sustainable and equitable economic development. The mining sector has suffered from corruption, instability, and a lack of transparency. Regardless, mining has remained a major source of employment and state revenue for the DRC (De Koning, 2011). The DRC—one of the world's poorest countries—ironically holds some of the world's greatest potential for wealth, with an estimated 24 trillion dollars' worth of available minerals buried in Congo's eastern hills (Wolfe, 2015).

The Minerals

The most significant minerals implicated in the DRC's conflict trade are gold, cassiterite, coltan, and wolframite, although they are more commonly known by the names of their extracted ores: gold, tin, tantalum, and tungsten (De Koning, 2011). These substances are in high demand, since they are the fundamental metals used often in modern-day technology like cameras, cellular phones, computers, and iPods. As expert John Prendergast explained, if a good has a circuit board, then it probably utilizes minerals from the DRC (Raj, 2011). Additionally, gold is commonly sought after by traders in Middle and Eastern Asia, where it is used to craft jewelry. (De Koning, 2011).

Gold. In 2012, the DRC was estimated to have the 10th highest reserves of gold in the world; however, current reserve figures are not available (KPMG Global Mining Institute [KPMG], 2014, p. 20). The 2014 *Democratic Republic of Congo: Country Mining Guide* from the KPMG Global Mining Institute offers a bit more insight to gold production, and their most recent estimated statistics show a production of 3,500 kg of gold in 2011—a significant drop from peak production of 12,400 kg in 2002 and 10,300 kg in 2006 (p. 28).

These numbers must be taken with a grain of salt, however, considering the growing popularity of gold in the Congolese black market in recent years. A 2014 report from the United Nations found that as much as 98% of all gold produced in the DRC is smuggled out of the nation, meaning that there is significant mining, production, and trade unaccounted for in official reports (Arieff, 2014). While other mineral outputs tend to be more easily accounted for, all official data regarding mineral production should still be viewed with the understanding that reports often do not represent complete statistics.

Tin. The DRC accounts for 3% of global tin production (KPMG, 2014, p. 20). While there are no current statistics on the nation's tin reserves, the DRC produced 3,000 t of tin in 2014 (U.S. Geological Survey [USGS], 2015). This places the DRC as the world's seventh greatest tin producer (KPMG, 2014, p. 2).

Tantalum. Reserve statistics on tantalum are also unavailable for the DRC; however, production statistics are available for the capital city of Kinshasa. In 2014, Kinshasa produced 180 t of tantalum, accounting for 28% of global tantalum production (USGS, 2015). These numbers qualify the DRC as the third largest producer of tantalum in the world (KPMG, 2014, p. 2).

Tungsten. No numbers are available regarding tungsten reserves in the DRC. However, the nation produced 800 t of tungsten in 2014 (USGS, 2015).

Other minerals. Gold, tin, tantalum, and tungsten are traditionally seen as the primary minerals implicated in conflict in the DRC but their mining and production in the DRC are actually marginal in comparison to the nation's most important minerals, which may also be associated with conflict: cobalt, copper, and diamonds (KPMG, 2014). The DRC accounts for 51% of the global cobalt production and is home to 41% of the world's cobalt reserves, with an estimated 3.4 million tonnes of cobalt in reserves at Kinshasa in 2014 (KPMG, 2014, p. 20).

Copper is another mineral that is of increasing importance in the Congolese mining sector. In 2014, it was estimated that the Kinshasa region had reserves of 20 million tonnes of copper (USGS, 2015). Despite enormous resources—the DRC has the world's largest undeveloped high-grade copper deposit—the DRC currently only accounts for 3% of global copper production, ranking it as the eighth highest copper producer in the world (KPMG, 2014, p. 2). However, the copper sector is expected to develop and largely drive growth in the next five years. Reserves at mines such as Kipoi and Kamoto are "estimated to contain [copper ore] grades above 3%, significantly higher than the world average of 0.6% - 0.8%" (KPMG, 2014, p. 2). This will be an important issue as some of the world's largest mines, including Antamina in Peru, Escondida in Chile, and Grasberg in Indonesia, have experienced falling ore grades and thus higher extraction costs (Business Monitor International [BMI], 2014).

The DRC also produces 25% of the world's diamonds (KPMG, 2014, p. 20), with industrial reserves at Kinshasa expected to hold 150 million carats (USGS, 2015). All of these minerals—gold, tin, tantalum, tungsten, cobalt, copper, and diamonds—have been implicated in the conflict mineral trade at some point or another, and they are probably not the only minerals that have been sourced under conditions of violence and illegal activity. However, literature surrounding the conflict mineral trade tends to only formally recognize the first four of these as "conflict minerals." Additionally, the Dodd-Frank Act (2010) defines conflict minerals as gold, tin, tantalum, and tungsten, which will be further discussed later on. It is important to recognize that while gold, tin, tantalum, and tungsten may be the most commonly implicated in conflict, they are not the only minerals subject to the conflict trade. In fact, all of the DRC's mineral resources have the potential to be involved in the conflict trade and therefore should be treated as such.

The Actors

Artisanal miners. It is difficult to determine how many artisanal miners are active in the DRC. Artisanal miners are independent, small-scale miners who usually spend long days under harsh conditions, digging through the mud with their hands and rudimentary tools in search of minerals. Modest estimates figure that artisanal mining employs approximately 450,000 people (De Koning, 2011); others suggest that at least 1 million people are active in artisanal mining (KPMG, 2014, p. 18). Others still point out that small-scale mining supports a wider community than those actually involved in mining activities, with some claims stating that artisanal mining provides direct or indirect support to more than 10 million people in the Congo (International Peace Information Service, 2013).

Unlike industrial mining, which is overseen by businessmen in air-conditioned offices and benefits from the convenience of heavy equipment, artisanal miners work on small-scale or independent levels, laboring long days under the sun with only their bare hands and rudimentary tools for assistance. Artisanal miners—along with other actors in the mining sector, including workers at militarized and industrialized mines—are subject to harsh working conditions. They are exposed to landslides, heavy metal inhalation, water contamination, monsoons, mercury, and prevalent child labor (KPMG, 2014, p. 18). It has been reported that up to 40% of all workers in the mining sector are children (KPMG, 2014, p. 18). The 1967 Labor Code, in compliance with suggestions made by the International Labor Organization, regulates labor guidelines concerning women, children, working conditions, and anti-discrimination, but "with the collapse of the economy and corruption in government, the enforcement of the code has been negatively affected" (KPMG, 2014, p. 18).

Artisanal mining is largely informal despite the 2002 Democratic Republic of Congo Mining Code stipulating guidelines and conditions for small-scale mining (International Peace Information Service, 2013).

The Directorate of Mines, a body formed to regulate mining activities with an emphasis on health, safety, and social issues, also issued a series of requirements for legal small-scale mining. The lengthy list of requirements includes obtaining an exploration license, a small-scale exploitation license, and the artisanal miner's card, among other provisions (BMI, 2014). However, most of these guidelines are not effectively enforced and thus are ignored by artisanal miners, who usually are not properly registered and perform mining activities on illegal property (International Peace Information Service, 2013).

Armed groups. There are numerous armed groups vying for power in the DRC. For most of these groups, money is power. Money provides the income needed to finance armies, purchase weapons, and conduct business deals or bribes. And, considering the economic influence of mines in the DRC, control of mines and minerals means money. Thus, mines mean power.

In July 2003, a transitional Congolese government was born out of the 2002 Global and Inclusive Peace Agreement, which laid a formal foundation for peace and was hoped to be the beginning of the end of conflict in the DRC (De Koning, 2011). However, the new government failed to bring "all rebel and militia groups under effective central command" (De Koning, 2011, p. 15), and as a result, fighting continued. There were—and still are—several main armies involved in perpetuating the fight. First is the *Forces Armées de la République Démocratique du Congo,* or the Armed Forces of the Democratic Republic of Congo (FARDC), which is the official national military. Then there is the *Forces démocratiques de libération du Rwanda,* the Democratic Forces for the Liberation of Rwanda (FDLR). The FDLR formed out of exiled Rwandan rebel groups which spilled across Congolese borders, and includes the Interahamwe responsible for perpetuating the Rwandan genocide along with other ethnic Hutus generally opposed to Tutsi rule (De Koning, 2011). The presence of the genocidaires deeply upset Congolese Tutsis, and remains a cause of resentment and tension to this day (Haskin, 2005).

The FDLR was also significant in that it shaped the mission of the *Congrès national pour la défense du peuple,* or the National Congress for the Defense of the People (CNDP). The CNDP was a political army formed by Laurent Nkunda in 2006 with the mission to protect Congolese Tutsis from the FDLR (Arieff, 2014). The CNDP has since been fractured and integrated into the FARDC, at least in the physical sense. In reality, however, the integration was not welcomed by all the soldiers and many retained their original military loyalties, thus making the integration effort a superficial one at best (De Koning, 2011). As a result, the FARDC remains today an army with deep internal divisions and very weak centralization.

Finally, there is the military presence of the Mai-Mai, or community-based militias. The Mai-Mai militias rose chiefly out of the need for locals to defend their communities against the influx of other armies, both national and foreign. While there have also been efforts to integrate the Mai-Mai into the FARDC, these efforts have been met with similarly limited success (De Koning, 2011).

All armed groups partake in the violent power struggle surrounding Congolese mines. Despite efforts to neutralize, demobilize, and stabilize armies in the DRC, there has been an upsurge of military violence in mineral rich areas, with many rebel armies staging retaliatory attacks on mines they've lost control over (De Koning, 2011). And the FARDC, which is meant to provide stability and security to the Congo, is not exempt from this behavior: it has poor governance and abusive tendencies. Its failure to consolidate security across the country has helped breed an environment where "state actors often appear more focused on controlling resources and augmenting their personal power than on establishing security, creating effective state institutions, and fostering socioeconomic development for the DRC's 75 million inhabitants" (Arieff, 2014).

As a whole, the military presence in the Congolese mining sector is a dangerous one. Militaries prey on civilian populations and are often implicated in mass lootings, killings, rapes, and illicit business operations (Arieff, 2014). The corruption of militaries and the ways in which they perpetuate conflict through the mining and trade of minerals will be addressed in further detail later on.

Industrial presence. Even though artisanal and alluvial miners account for most of the operations in the Congolese mining sector, there are still a number of state-owned, domestic and foreign companies at play. The industrial presence in mining remains relatively small, however, because of the high-risk business environment in the DRC. In 2013, the World Bank's *Doing Business* report ranked the DRC as 181 out of 185 countries, placing it as one of the worst nations in the world with which to engage in business (Arieff, 2014). Private sector development faces a large range of obstacles in the Congo, "including underdeveloped infrastructure, inadequate contract enforcement, limited access to credit, continued insecurity in the east, inadequate property rights protection, high levels of bureaucratic red tape and corruption, and a lack of reliable electricity" (Arieff, 2014, p. 128). The DRC poses so many concerns and risks when it comes to business operations that many multinational corporations are subsequently discouraged from investment, and, in recent years, due diligence laws have further decreased international incentive to get involved in the Congolese mining sector. This phenomenon will be further expanded upon in later sections of this paper.

Nevertheless, there is still a large-scale industrial presence in the DRC. The mining of gold is dominated principally by two corporations: Randgold Resources and AngloGold Ashanti, which own and operate the Kibali mine (BMI, 2014). While not as dominant as Randgold and Anglogold, the Banro Corporation also accounts for a portion of the gold sector, and the rest of the sector is mostly composed of artisanal miners (BMI, 2014). Copper mines in the DRC are also highly diversified, with major international and domestic players being Tenke Fungurume Mining, Katanga Mining, Freeport, Glencore Xstrata, Anvil Mining, and Chemaf (BMI, 2014). The diamond sector is similarly diversified, with one-third of its production overseen by the state and the other two-thirds left to alluvial mining (BMI, 2014). The industrial presence is also felt in the silver and iron ore sectors of mining. As for other sectors, however, such as tin, it seems that large corporations are more hesitant to get their hands dirty. As a result, most mining in the remaining sectors is either carried out in militarized mines or by artisanal miners (BMI, 2014).

While there seems to be hesitancy to engage in private sector development in the DRC—not only because of business risks, but also out of fear of being implicated in human rights abuses—there are still areas of the world willing to establish trade relations with the Congo. One such area is China, which has an investment track record that has been more forgiving of human rights violations and unjust business practices than other countries. This stance, combined with a mining landscape relatively free of international competition, has led to the supposition that China will become a major actor in the field of Congolese mineral extraction in coming years (BMI, 2014). And in fact, increased Chinese investment in the DRC is already occurring. China has been drawn to the Congo for its large quantities of untapped resources, low mining costs, and the fact that the West's relative abandonment of Congo in the mineral trade has left doors wide open for Chinese businessmen (Lee, 2010).

The Process and Its Problems

It is important to know the actors involved in the DRC's mining sector. However, it is also important to know the trade process and understand the steps involved in getting the minerals from the actors into the hands of global manufacturers. After extraction, minerals and ores usually first come into contact with *petits négociants*, or small-scale intermediaries.

These intermediaries have either pre-financed extraction operations—by trading equipment in exchange for minerals—or simply buy the minerals outright, in order to then sell them to trading chains (De Koning, 2011). The traders who purchase the minerals from the small-scale intermediaries are known as *négociants*. They, in turn, sell the minerals to buying houses called *comptoirs*, which arrange exports to manufacturers (De Koning, 2011). Minerals are transported along trade routes either by road or by air (De Koning, 2011).

This process sounds very neat and orderly when laid out so simply on paper. However, in truth the official mineral trade is anything but organized and efficient. It is rampant with difficulties, corruption, and conflict, and is severely undermined by demand from black markets and home refineries. The most popular mineral in underground trade is gold, which has a high value by volume, meaning that valuable, exportable quantities can be concealed easily (De Koning, 2011). It is estimated that $1.24 billion worth of gold is smuggled out of the DRC each year (De Koning, 2011). It is hard to regulate such illegal exports of minerals, since many traders and buying houses own private airlines and road transport companies, which are often used to transport minerals and allegedly facilitate smuggling (De Koning, 2011). Likewise, public efforts to improve Congolese infrastructure and develop road systems have ironically made it more and more difficult to trace and control illegal exports of conflict minerals.

Militaries also engage in and directly benefit from this illicit trade. Low pay combined with a corrupt and unfair military payroll generates incentive for militiamen to seek other means of income—namely, by smuggling and trading minerals illegally (De Koning, 2011). On a larger scale, mineral profits are used to fund entire armed groups. Unlawful profits from tin, tantalum, tungsten, and gold collectively funded armies an approximated $185 million in 2008, and gold alone is estimated to bring in an annual $44 million to $88 million to militaries (Raj, 2011). These profits are used to buy more weapons in order to impose a "brutal form of order" (Raj, 2011, p. 989) upon a population already ravaged by disease, poverty, and civil war.

Aside from the black market, state and non-state actors alike are involved in underhanded business deals, such as underpricing assets and refusing to pay taxes, duties, and fines (Arieff, 2014). One such example can be found by observing the complex deals involving offshore companies and two multinational companies, Glencote and Eurasian Natural Resources Corporation. Investigations have shown that the companies have ties to President Kabila, although specifics on the exact nature of these ties remain vague. Nevertheless, this relationship suggests a conflict of interest, perhaps even that the Congolese President is benefiting from the sale of conflict minerals and, as a result, may also have a decreased incentive to end the conflict mineral trade (Arieff, 2014).

Actors in the conflict mineral trade also frequently partake in tax fraud. Mining authorities, such as commanding militaries, often levy unofficial taxes and traders in order to reap personal profit. These taxes can vary greatly, ranging from as little as the equivalent of $5 a week to the equivalent of $3,000 a week (De Koning, 2011). Such levies can be applied at any point in the production and trade chain. This exploitation is also more regularly found in mines that experience frequent shifts in ownership (De Koning, 2011).

Many miners, militias, small-scale intermediaries, and traders also organize lootings of mining sites and villages. These raids not only provide immediate profit gain, but also breed insecurity to discourage the return of refugees, disrupt the FARDC deployments, and eliminate commercial competitors from the commodity chain (De Koning, 2011). Lootings occur most frequently in the Walikale territory and are most often perpetuated by the Mai-Mai Sheka (De Koning, 2011). While the FARDC does not participate in lootings as frequently—since they are supposed to protect the Congolese people, not attack them—they are not guilt-free. It is difficult to distinguish the number of lootings perpetuated by the FARDC, because when national soldiers attack villages they often disguise their identity to escape punishment by the national army (De Koning, 2011). Whoever the perpetrator, these raids leave the civilian population scattered, terrorized, and impoverished.

Desire for mine control and mineral profits has also been shown to fuel a culture of rape and sexual violence in the DRC. Sexual violence is "used as a systematic weapon of war in the Democratic Republic of Congo to subjugate and humiliate civilians in regions under militia control" (Raj, 2011, p. 990). Human Rights Watch has estimated that since 1998, tens of thousands of women—if not hundreds of thousands—have fallen victim to sadistic rapes (Raj, 2011). Although no militia is truly exempt from the violence, many of the rapes have been inflicted by Rwandan genocidaires, the majority of whom are never brought to justice and instead continue to "roam with impunity and continue in positions of power through mineral profits" (Raj, 2011, p. 990). Thus, the Congo has been labeled "the most dangerous place on earth to be a woman" (Raj, 2011, p. 989). Relatedly, the country also came in dead last on the 2013 U.N. Human Development Index (Arieff, 2014).

While in no way does all this conflict stem from mining, it is not a coincidence that violence is concentrated in North and South Kivu, as well as the Orientale, the Congolese provinces containing the greatest mineral wealth (Raj, 2011). In 2011, it was estimated that 45,000 Congolese die every month as a result of ongoing conflict, which amounts to about 1,500 preventable deaths a day (Raj, 2011). Additionally, there are over 2.6 million Congolese displaced internally, with an additional 500,000 Congolese refugees seeking shelter in border countries (Arieff, 2014). Raj (2011) adds:

> the dimensions of conflict in eastern DR Congo range from internal to regional power struggles to tensions over identity, ethnicity, and resources...it is equally undeniable that the multimillion dollar global minerals trade is one of the central issues fueling the conflict and the corresponding humanitarian crisis. Though mineral wealth did not cause the original war in DR Congo, the mineral trade sustains armed combatants and fuels ongoing atrocities. (p. 985)

ANTI-CONFLICT MINERAL LEGISLATION

International Response

A growing international awareness of the conflict in the Congo in recent years has sparked outrage and a call for action. Many countries, such as the United States, have decided to organize legislation, frameworks, and sanctions against the trade of conflict minerals, with an aim for peace, transparency, and accountability.

Perhaps one of the earliest anti-conflict mineral initiatives was birthed in 2003, with the creation of the Kimberley Process. The Kimberley Process Certification Scheme was adopted by forty countries involved in the diamond industry, as well as the World Diamond Council and two NGOs, Global Witness and Partnership Africa Canada (Lecomte, 2014). This public-private partnership aims to eradicate conflict minerals via export bans. Its framework outlines the Kimberley Process's governing authoritative bodies, organization and decision-making structures, responsibilities for monitoring performance, and guidelines for public disclosure (Lecomte, 2014). While the Kimberley Process remains in place today, it has achieved mixed results and received harsh criticism because of its voluntary nature, self-policing, inadequate monitoring, administrative structure, consensus system of decision-making, and lack of independent supervision (Nanda, 2014). And similar to other anti-conflict mineral legislation, the Kimberley Process has had difficulty maintaining legitimacy due to corruption and smuggling (Rhode, 2014).

Since then, there have been other international movements to stop the conflict mineral trade. In 2013, the European Trade Commissioner, Karel De Gucht, claimed that the European Union had developed a successful initiative on responsible mineral sourcing, and he pledged that the European Union would "help keep money out of the hands of rebel groups" (Nanda, 2014, p. 287), and "help ensure that revenues from natural resources instead go to the government, strengthening the rule of law and improving the provision of vital services like health and education" (Nanda, 2014, p. 287). Canada is also responding to the Congolese conflict. In 2013, they issued a "private member's bill" (Nanda, 2014, p. 300) that addressed issues of mineral extraction, processing, purchase, trade, and use.

There have also been efforts within the DRC itself to remedy conflict mineral violence. For instance, the International Conference on the Great Lakes Region (ICGLR)—an intergovernmental organization including both the DRC and Rwanda—created a mineral certification process titled the ICGLR Regional Initiative Against the Exploitation of Natural Resources (Nanda, 2014). Its Regional Certification Mechanism (RCM) has four components: mine inspection and traceability, the creation of a regional mineral tracking database, audits, and independent monitoring, although the implementation of the latter two requirements has not been finalized (Nanda, 2014). Despite this legislation, however, governments in the Great Lakes Region of Africa have failed to uphold the mineral certification process (Nanda, 2014).

The Organisation for Economic Cooperation and Development (OECD) has also been instrumental in creating an international framework for the regulation and trade of conflict minerals. In 2011, the member nations of the OECD revised existing international guidelines regarding corporate behavior to promote more stringent principles in defense of human rights. One of the new guidelines introduced during revisions was Due Diligence Guidance, which builds off of the general principle of due diligence and supply chain provisions already existing in the OECD Guidelines for Multinational Enterprises (Nanda, 2014). The Due Diligence Guidance implicated not only the OECD, but also the United Nations, the governments of the Great Lakes Region of Africa, the business community, and several civil society groups (Nanda, 2014). The OECD (2013) guidelines state that its mission is to:

> help companies respect human rights and avoid contributing to conflict through sourcing decisions…[to] help companies contribute to sustainable development and source responsibly from conflict-affected and high-risk areas, while creating the enabling conditions for constructive engagement with suppliers. (p. 12)

OECD guidelines of due diligence apply to every company that uses conflict minerals, regardless of their placement on the supply chain. However, the framework does specify that due diligence should be tailored to the individual company depending on matters such as the size of the enterprise, its location, situation, and the nature of the products produced (Nanda, 2014). While the customization of due diligence requirements is important, it can also be problematic: on an economic note, it is more expensive to evaluate each company and personalize a due diligence plan for it. Customization could also be problematic, however, because it may create the opportunity for loopholes. Without some universal standard requirement concerning mineral sourcing, companies may begin slipping through the cracks.

There are four main sections of the *OECD Due Diligence Guidance*: a detailing of the overarching due diligence structure, an example of a mineral supply chain policy, suggestions for risk mitigation and indicators for measuring improvement, and two supplements on conflict minerals, specifically designed to address the challenges associated with the supply chain structures of tin, tantalum, tungsten, and gold (OECD, 2013). In terms of the actual due diligence process itself, the OECD outlines a five step process. First, strong company management systems must be established. In order to do so, the OECD suggests improved communication with suppliers as well as the public, increased transparency, and a company- or industry-wide grievance system (OECD, 2013). Second, risk in conflict mineral supply chains must be identified and assessed (OECD, 2013). Third, companies must design and implement a strategy to respond to the formerly identified risks. Such a strategy should include reporting risk assessment findings, devising and implementing a risk management plan, and completing supplementary risk assessments for those requiring mitigation (OECD, 2013). Fourth, companies should complete third-party audits of supply chain due diligence at specified points along the supply chain (OECD, 2013). Finally, companies should submit a report on their supply chain due diligence policies (OECD, 2013).

Additionally, several international industries have also responded to the crisis in the Congo. For instance, in 2012 the World Gold Council implemented the Conflict-Free Gold Standard to assess gold extraction, with a focus on financial transparency, human rights protection, and creating a justice system of reporting and revolving infringements (Nanda, 2014). Another industry group that has taken a stand against the conflict mineral trade is the Responsible Jewelry Council (RJC). The RJC places an emphasis on jewelers upholding "responsible standards" (Nanda, 2014, p. 301) for mining and buying gold and diamonds.

U.S. Response

The United States is arguably one of the world's most influential countries in terms of advocating for peace in the DRC, in terms of both its aid programs and its legislation. U.S. annual bilateral aid to the Congo totaled between $200 million and $300 million in recent years, not including an additional $50 million to $150 million of annual emergency aid and another $400 million to $600 million in annual contributions to the U.N. Organization Stabilization Operation in the Democratic Republic of Congo (Arieff, 2014).

Apart from the Office of Detainee Affairs, the U.S. wields its influence via legislation and foreign policy, most notably Section 1502 of the Dodd-Frank Act. Before delving into the Dodd-Frank Act, however, it is important to note some lesser examples of

Congressional action regarding the Congo. The U.S. Congress has taken several routes to deter corruption and conflict in the DRC: restricting bilateral aid to the Congo when militaristic state-backed forces misbehave, such as by employing child soldiers or failing to appropriately respond to human trafficking; restricting government-to-government assistance when the DRC fails to uphold budgetary transparency; authorizing targeted sanctions against dangerous rebel persons; and restricting military aid to Rwanda if the government is caught supporting rebel groups (Arieff, 2014). In past years, the U.S. has also been involved in facilitating peace accords in the Great Lakes Region of Africa (Arieff, 2014).

These actions aside, the most important—and globally influential—piece of U.S. legislation regarding the Congo in recent years is Section 1502 of the Dodd-Frank Act. Not only has this act impacted life in the Congo significantly—the impacts of which will be examined in the next section—it has also served as legislative inspiration for other nations, such as the European Union, who have strived to imitate it (Nanda, 2014). The regulations set forth in the Dodd-Frank Act were issued by the Securities and Exchange Commission and were made official when the act was signed into federal law in July 2010 (Nanda, 2014). In the most simplified sense, the Dodd-Frank Act simply requires that companies disclose whether or not the minerals used—or contracted to be used—to create their goods and services have been implicated in conflict in the DRC (Nanda, 2014). The Dodd-Frank Act (2010) begins by putting Congressional concerns front and center:

> It is the sense of Congress that the exploitation and trade of conflict minerals originating in the Democratic Republic of the Congo is helping to finance conflict characterized by extreme levels of violence in the eastern Democratic Republic of the Congo, particularly sexual- and gender-based violence, and contributing to an emergency humanitarian situation therein. (p. 838)

These concerns are the foundation of the Act's due diligence framework. According to the Dodd-Frank Act, companies must determine if minerals originated in the DRC or an adjoining country, and if so, they must then submit a report to the SEC (Dodd-Frank Act, 2010). In turn, this report must contain several key pieces of information. First, there must be a description of the due diligence measures undertaken by the company that includes a certified private sector audit, which simply means that an impartial third party must come in to evaluate how well the company executed their mineral sourcing. The report must also include a description of the products manufactured or expected to be manufactured with minerals that are not conflict free, including the minerals' country of origin, the processing facilities used to mine them, and the efforts taken to source them (Dodd-Frank Act, 2010).

The second part of Section 1502 requires the Secretary of State to devise a strategy "to address the linkages between human rights abuses, armed groups, mining of conflict minerals, and commercial products" (Dodd-Frank Act, 2010, p. 840). The plan must focus on supporting the Congolese government in its pursuit of peace and security, with special emphasis on monitoring and ceasing commercial activity that contributes to violence and human rights abuses, as well as a devotion to creating stronger institutions and governance to improve trade facilitation and transparency (Dodd-Frank Act, 2010). Additionally, the plan should guide companies seeking to exercise due diligence and describe punitive measures that will be inflicted upon groups failing to comply with the Act's mission of peace and human rights (Dodd-Frank Act, 2010).

Under Section 1502, the Secretary of State is also responsible for creating a map—the Conflict Minerals Map—that details "mineral-rich zones, trade routes, and areas under the control of armed groups in the Democratic Republic of the Congo and adjoining countries based on data from multiple sources" (Dodd-Frank Act, 2010, p. 841). The map must be regularly updated, released to the public, and used by Congress (Dodd-Frank Act, 2010).

The next sub-section of the Dodd-Frank Act details a multitude of reports to be made by Comptroller General of the United States in order to determine both the effectiveness of Section 1502 and to maintain accountability of its due diligence process. The necessary reports include a baseline report that assesses the rate of sexual- and gender-based violence in the Congo and adjoining nations, a "regular report on effectiveness" (Dodd-Frank Act, 2010, p. 841)—which includes information such as any problems encountered when implementing the Act—and a report on private sector auditing, which both assesses the current audits and makes recommendations for improvements in future audits (Dodd-Frank Act, 2010).

The final section of the Dodd-Frank Act deals with technicalities and definitions. Perhaps the most important definition presented in this section is that of "conflict mineral," which includes the expected gold, tin, tantalum, and tungsten, but also leaves some leeway to include other potentially problematic minerals:

The term "conflict mineral" means (a) columbite-tantalite (coltan), cassiterite, gold, wolframite, or their derivatives; or (b) any other mineral or its derivatives determined by the Secretary of State to be financing conflict in the Democratic Republic of the Congo or an adjoining country. (Dodd-Frank Act, 2010, p. 843)

EVALUATION OF ANTI-CONFLICT MINERAL LEGISLATION

Anti-conflict mineral legislation was passed with the intention to terminate the trade of conflict minerals, stem the flow of income to armed actors in the Congo, and thus help end the violence and conflict in the DRC. While peace may have been the motivation behind much of this legislation, the question now stands: has peace been the outcome of such legislation? Using the Dodd-Frank Act as a case study, this section will seek to understand the real-life implications of anti-conflict mineral legislation in the DRC. In particular, this section will explore claims that the Dodd-Frank Act has hurt, not helped, the Congo.

First and foremost, it is important to note that the Dodd-Frank Act is a piece of legislation that operates in accordance with the notion that greed serves as a cause of civil war. This is a notion that was championed by scholars Paul Collier and Anke Hoeffler, whose work will be discussed later on. In short, however, the argument claims that rebellions and armed conflicts occur out of a desire on the part of combatants to profit, and that combatants will seize any opportunities for self-enrichment (Collier & Hoeffler, 2004). The Dodd-Frank Act tries to counteract the greed motivation by limiting profit opportunities for armed groups, namely by discouraging the purchase of conflict minerals through due diligence and mineral sourcing.

Legislators saw such due diligence reports as a step that could simply be inserted into the trade chains of tin, tantalum, tungsten and gold. What they did not foresee, however, was how implanting due diligence reports into the middle of trade chains would change other steps and processes along the chain. The U.S. Securities and Exchange Commission estimated that it could cost companies an annual $71 million to implement due diligence measures such as database tracking, on-site mine monitoring and multiple audits; the National Association of Manufacturers put forth even greater expense estimates, ranging between $9 billion and $16 billion dollars per company per year (Drajem, Hamilton & Kavanagh, 2011). Instead of these expenditures simply being an added measure in the trade chain, they actually worked to alter trade altogether. These expenses incentivized many multinational companies to completely pull out of the DRC due to the belief that the costs of participating in Congolese trade outweighed any benefits (Drajem et al., 2004). For instance, even without the added expense of due diligence reports, the DRC does not offer a very hospitable business environment to foreign corporations: it suffers from lack of transparency, risks of violence and corruption, and the threat of companies being implicated in human rights violations and suffering consequently tarnished reputations. One example is the case of Malaysia Smelting, one of the largest global tin producers, which had previously purchased 80% of the DRC's tin (Wolfe, 2015). After the passing of anti-conflict mineral legislation, Malaysia Smelting entirely stopped purchasing Congolese ore out of the fear of "being labeled a user of conflict minerals" (Wolfe, 2015).

Yet even for companies that maintained business relations in the Congo despite new compliance costs, due diligence reports were still not necessarily a booming success. Some companies simply did not make conflict-free mineral sourcing a serious priority—most notably, car and plane manufacturers

"stood back and refused to use their buying power to bring change" (Propper & Knight, 2013). But even companies that were sincerely concerned with the crisis in the Congo had difficulty determining the legitimacy of their minerals, oftentimes through no fault of their own. There have been many criticisms regarding the difficulty of proving mineral legitimacy in the DRC: lack of regulation on federal and local levels, a cumbersome certification process, poor infrastructure, and turbulent conditions on-site (Propper & Knight, 2013). For instance, according to Adalbert Murhi Mubalama—the minister of mines in the South Kivu province—companies cannot even audit mines in Shabunda territory, where most mines are located, because the land is controlled by a ruthless militia (Raghavan, 2014). So ruthless is this militia that, according to Mubalama, the Congolese government cannot even enter the territory (Raghavan, 2014).

Besides a chaotic environment and inefficient bureaucracy, there have also been issues on the scientific and technical levels with regards to the fingerprinting conflict minerals. Immediately after mining, mineral ores are processed to become ore concentrates—that is, small, granular bits of powder. During this process, ores from different mines are often mixed together, meaning that ores from conflict-free mines may very well be mixed with ores from conflict mines (Arnaud, 2012). The mixed ores are then smelted together—a process that extracts metal from the ores via heating and melting—and "after the metal has been extracted from the ore, there may be no way to determine provenance" (Arnaud, 2012, p. 37). This means that if multinational companies trace their minerals back to smelters—such as in the cases of Apple and Intel—they have no real way to prove that their minerals are conflict-free, because all the ores have been melted together (An Open Letter, 2014). This means that companies may very well have purchased a metal mixture containing both conflict and conflict-free minerals. There are movements in the science community to develop technology to geochemically fingerprint minerals, which would mean being able to determine mineral origins even after smelting, such as laser-induced breakdown spectroscopy (Arnaud, 2012). However, even this burgeoning technology is viewed skeptically by many scholars, who remain unconvinced that such techniques will be affordable, realistic, or even capable of providing suitable mineral fingerprints for due diligence purposes (Arnaud, 2012).

There are further issues with fingerprinting conflict minerals. There is a serious lack of transparency in the overall trade of minerals, which makes it exceedingly difficult if not impossible to track minerals to their true origin. For example, many of the Congo's minerals are sent across national borders to Rwanda, where they are then processed and sold to multinational companies (De Koning, 2011). However, Rwanda registers any minerals processed in the country under their own country of origin (De Koning, 2011). As a result, companies may be buying processed minerals from Rwanda believing they were sourced there in conflict-free conditions, when in reality the minerals were mined under conditions of violence in the Congo and simply washed clean by some manipulative paperwork that alters their country of origin.

Because of all these difficulties surrounding mineral legitimacy, with the passing of the Dodd-Frank Act in 2010, many corporations pulled out of business investments in the Congo (Drajem et al., 2011). At the very least, most traders delayed mineral purchases until they could vouch for their origins (Drajem et al., 2011). What resulted was a de facto embargo on mining in the DRC (Gallo, 2011). At the same time, in September 2010, the Congolese government issued "a six-month ban on all mining and trading activities in the East" (Gettleman, 2013). Only two months after the Dodd-Frank Act had been signed into law, mineral production had ceased even at mining facilities not operated by armed groups (Raghavan, 2014). The combination of the de facto embargo and the de jure mining ban had resulted in the Congolese mining and trade sector shuddering to a halt and the obliteration of local economies (Drajem et al., 2011).

The official ban was lifted six months later in March 2011, but by then the damage was already done and its aftershocks were clearly visible in the DRC economically and socially. Official mining businesses did not recuperate well. Many artisanal mines simply never re-opened and legal mineral exports did not bounce back to the same levels as before the ban. For instance, by April 2011, legal tantalum exports from the DRC had dropped by more than 90%, bringing legitimate tantalum production to a near stand-

still (Drajem et al., 2011). Another example can be seen in the region of Luntukulu, which used to be a hotspot for international mineral trade, with scores of businessmen flocking there each year to purchase minerals for smelting. In 2014, however, only 12 buyers made an appearance, according to community leaders (Raghavan, 2014). Many of these buyers were from India and China, where the Dodd-Frank Act has no jurisdiction (Raghavan, 2014). The sudden loss of Western clients reverberated throughout the Luntukulu community: shops closed, families went hungry, and miners bitterly blamed what they call "Loi Obama"—Obama's Law (Raghavan, 2014).

The boycott of Congolese minerals did not just have a microeconomic impact on regions such as Luntukulu, however; it also made an impression in a macroeconomic sense, negatively affecting Congolese exports in the global arena. When foreign companies began to avoid buying minerals from the DRC, the international prices of Congolese minerals were driven down. For example, before the passing of the Dodd-Frank Act, Congolese miners could receive $7 per kg of tin (Raghavan, 2014). This number was still dramatically underpriced compared to the rest of the world market for tin, in which most countries could receive $18 per kg (Raghavan, 2014). After the Dodd-Frank Act came into play, this price gap only grew. In 2014, Congolese miners could expect to receive the equivalent of $4 per kg of tin, even though the world market price for tin was now worth $22 per kg (Raghavan, 2014).

The good news is that while the DRC's economy suffered, the income and authority of armed groups in the Congo suffered too. Some reports estimate that nearly 10% of mines in Eastern Congo have been declared "clean," meaning that they are now demilitarized (Gettleman, 2013). However, these same reports are careful to note that even though these mines may be officially demilitarized, it does not necessarily mean they are free of conflict, as many of these clean mines still reside in territories controlled by armed groups or rebels (Gettleman, 2013).

Another study put forth by the Enough Project offers even more optimistic findings, claiming that the Dodd-Frank Act actually achieved its goal of decreasing the presence of armed groups in the Congo's mines. According to this study, which was produced from five months of field research, armed groups have lost control of nearly two-thirds of the mining sites they previously presided over (Wolfe, 2015). However, some critics have argued that "the assertion that any decrease was due to Dodd-Frank…is impossible to prove" (Wolfe, 2015), and suggest that the Enough Project's study may make the error of mistaking correlation for causation, although they do not provide any insight into what other causes may be. Other research similarly confirms a de-militarization of mines, although progress admittedly seems to be slow and unstable. As of June 2014, it was reported that twenty five mining sites in South and North Kivu were declared "green"—meaning no armed groups, children, or pregnant laborers were employed—but this is still a minor fraction out of hundreds of mines in the region (Raghavan, 2014). And as of October 2014, 11 mines in South Kivu had been declared completely conflict free (Raghavan, 2014). This is an honorable feat, though with an approximated 900 mines present in South Kivu, there is clearly still a great deal of work to be done (Raghavan, 2014).

Still, it is significant to note that armed groups saw their profits from conflict minerals drop after the passing of the Dodd-Frank Act. One report claims that "armed groups that were trading in tin, tantalum, and tungsten saw their profits drop by sixty five percent" (Gettleman, 2013). However, it is equally important to note that these profit decreases were not massive enough to significantly deter conflict in the Congo. This is for a variety of reasons. The first reason is that armed groups were never solely dependent on mineral revenue for their existence; therefore, they are able to continue existing even without monetary aid from minerals (Wolfe, 2015). Many militias simply turned to other trades to make up the difference in lack of income, trades of such items as charcoal, marijuana, palm oil, soap, and various consumer goods (*An Open Letter*, 2014). Many non-state militias also simply resorted to kidnapping and extortion as major sources of income (Gallo, 2011).

Furthermore, many illegal exports were able to continue even after the mining ban, thanks to a thriving black market, as well as a stockpile of mineral resources in the possession of armed groups (De Koning, 2011). Although it is difficult to track the financial specifics of the black market, there are many

ways to surmise evidence of illegal activity across African borders. Take for instance recent export statistics from Uganda and Burundi. In the last decade, as the DRC's exports decreased, Uganda and Burundi's exports have dramatically increased. In their peak year of 2006, Burundi and Uganda exported over 4.5 t and 7 t of gold respectively, even though both countries had "negligible domestic production capacities" (De Koning, 2011, p. 11). Based on the difference between the countries' domestic production capacities and their actual export quotas, it is estimated that "over ten tonnes of gold must have arrived in Burundi and Uganda from elsewhere in 2006. The DRC is the most likely source" (De Koning, 2011, p. 11). Thus, while it is commendable that the profits of armed groups have decreased, this loss of income has not led to a disbandment of armed groups and decrease of conflict, as legislators hoped. Furthermore, what little strides have been made in decreasing the profits of armed groups seem to be offset by the massive costs of the Dodd-Frank Act, namely the economic and humanitarian damage incurred by the Congo.

Such humanitarian damage is also an important consequence to take into account when considering the relative failure of the Dodd-Frank Act. Negative ripple effects from the Dodd-Frank Act can clearly be seen in the global and Congolese economies, but its effects are not limited strictly to fiscal matters—its damage has also extended to Congolese society to create a humanitarian crisis. When the mining and trade sector collapsed, so did the livelihoods of the Congolese. It is estimated that between 5 million to 12 million Congolese were either directly or indirectly impacted by the unemployment created by the mining ban and the aftershocks it produced (Wolfe, 2015). The sudden lack of income meant deficiency in medical care, children dropping out of school, and widespread starvation and malnutrition (Gallo, 2011).

But perhaps the most disconcerting social impact of the Dodd-Frank Act was the way it almost served to help, not hurt, armed groups in the DRC. Widespread unemployment stemmed from the complicated reality that resources that may have funded armed conflict simultaneously "provide[d] livelihoods to many people who work in and around artisanal mines" (De Koning, 2011, p. 3). Thus, by cutting off income for armed groups, more often than not income is also prevented from reaching legitimate, peaceful, independent miners. Many miners are being forced to find other ways to survive and have resorted to joining armed groups or smuggling rackets for quick income and a greater sense of protection (*An Open Letter*, 2014). This is, in the most literal sense, a complete backfire of the Dodd-Frank Act's intentions—a piece of legislation that was meant to disband Congolese armed groups is, in some instances, actually reinforcing their numbers. Furthermore, it is not only the former miners that join, but also sometimes children, and this creates an even greater problem: the children in question fail to receive an education and ultimately reinforce a historic cycle of knowledge poverty and militarized violence (Raghavan, 2014).

RELEVANT LITERATURE

In light of the failure of the Dodd-Frank Act, the work of three scholars—Paul Collier, Anke Hoeffler, and William Reno—emerges as especially relevant and insightful in understanding the crisis in the DRC. First is Collier's work, which discusses the political and economic consequences of natural resources. Collier (2010) presents what he calls the "resource curse" (pp. 1106-1107), a term that he uses to describe nations possessing vast quantities of valuable natural resources, such as the Congo. According to Collier (2010), the resource curse can undermine both security and accountability within a nation. Furthermore, the more valuable the resources are, the less likely it is that a civil war occurring in that nation will be settled, as there is greater opportunity for profit-seeking and greed (Collier, 2010).

According to Collier (2010), there are three ways that the resource curse contributes to civil wars. First, profits from commodity exports "provide opportunities for rebel predation during conflict and so can finance the escalation and sustainability of rebellion" (p. 1111). Second, not only will such profit-earning opportunities simply be made feasible, but rebels may actually be motivated to seize income (Collier, 2010). Finally, governments of countries with vast resource wealth tend to be less accountable to their citizens, and thus less capable of preventing conflict (Collier, 2010). All three consequences of the resource curse can clearly be seen in the current state of the Congo.

Important work is also put forth by Reno, particularly a study which looks at the behavior of armed groups and patronage politics. Reno (2007) describes armed groups as "agents of disorder" (p. 324) that are often vulnerable to collaboration with "predatory politicians, international criminals and local gangsters who occupy positions of power in failing states" (p. 324). He explains that armed groups can play one of two roles in a civil war: predator or protectorate (Collier, 2010). Reno may make this binary a bit too clearly defined, however. As is evident in the Congo, sometimes the roles of armed groups are not so black-and-white. The FARDC, for instance, is supposed to protect Congolese citizens, but often ends up exploiting them as much as any rebel army.

Nevertheless, Reno (2007) points out that predatory armed groups make wars longer and more violent as they vie for control of local communities and exploit natural resources. People who join these groups often do so to "increase their status and gain a measure of greater personal security" (Reno, 2007, p. 324), a motive that was clearly at play when unemployed artisanal miners in the Congo decided to begin joining armed groups after the mining ban and embargo. Reno (2007) also makes note of the fact that "the most predatory and socially destabilizing violence should develop in areas where the political establishment was most closely linked to the patronage networks of the capital" (p. 337), pointing towards a type of corruption that has corroded modern Congolese politics.

Finally, work by Collier and Hoeffler presents the debate over the motivation of civil wars: greed or grievance? While it could be argued that both play significant roles in breeding dissent, Collier and Hoeffler make a strong case for greed over grievance. They cite three opportunities for conflict that are created by greed. First is the availability of finance: the idea that "primary commodity exports substantially increase conflict risk" (Collier & Hoeffler, 2010, p. 588), because the greater quantity and quality of exports a nation has, the more potential for profit it offers to armed groups, and thus the incentive to defect is greater. Second is the cost of rebellion; in nations where the costs of rebellion are higher, such as greater rates of secondary male education, per capita income, and growth, the less likely civil war becomes (Collier & Hoeffler, 2010). In nations like the DRC, however, where there is lower quality of life, combatants have less to lose and more to gain by rebellion. Finally, there is military advantage: the idea that in countries with dispersed populations, militaries will better be able to seize control of local communities, and thus conflict will increase (Collier & Hoeffler, 2010). This, too, is evident in the Congo—a vast territory with a weak centralized government is the perfect recipe for rebellious armed groups to seize and conquer.

In reviewing the works of these three authors, the complexities at play in the Congo become a bit more clearly defined in the light of modern political theories. In fact, in many ways the Congo stands as a perfect case study in support of these claims—their resources have bred conflict, armed groups have increased citizen insecurity, and greed has contributed to civil war. However, the failure of the Dodd-Frank Act may also suggest that in some ways, the Congo isn't actually a perfect fit with these theories. After all, the Dodd-Frank Act targeted two main sources of civil war as according to these scholars: the resource curse and greed. Despite this, the Dodd-Frank Act failed to end conflict in the Congo. Perhaps this failure suggests that greed is not the greatest driving factor behind civil war. Maybe in the Congo or elsewhere, grievances—such as issues of citizenship, politics, and ethnicity—can sometimes trump greed, or at least play equally significant roles in driving conflict, and should be similarly addressed in legislation.

Solutions for Peace

Anti-conflict mineral legislation, the Dodd-Frank Act in particular, was passed with intentions to create stability and peace in the DRC. Yet much of this same legislation did little to encourage either and, in some instances, actually actively worked against a mission of peace.

So where does this paradox leave us? Global leaders tried to cure the problem but instead aggravated it. So is there any real solution to the crisis in the Congo? While there may not be one miraculous panacea, there are some improvements that could be made in the way in which foreign policy understands and handles the Congolese crisis, which may ultimately lead to more successful means of achieving peace.

First and foremost, there needs to be reform in the way global leaders understand the crisis in the DRC. As is, legislators seem to have a very limited, shallow—and therefore, seriously flawed—understanding of what exactly is happening in the Congo. *An Open Letter*, published in 2014 and signed by seventy scholars, politicians, and civil society authorities, claimed that "the conflict minerals campaign fundamentally misunderstands the relationship between minerals and conflict in the eastern DRC" (p. 1). Legislators have been criticized for having a grievously one-dimensional understanding of the conflict for thinking of conflict minerals as being directly and solely responsible for humanitarian abuses. They oversimplify the conflict by believing that "iPhones cause rape" and "shiny things fuel war" (Wolfe, 2015). This sort of belief is problematic because it presents an understanding of the relationship between Congolese minerals and Congolese conflict that is too narrow, and this incomplete understanding in turn leads to limited or ineffective conflict resolutions.

This is not to say that conflict minerals and the consumer goods that utilize them do not play a role in the conflict. They undeniably do. However, to reduce conflict in the Congo merely to tin, tantalum, tungsten, and gold is to disregard the multitude of nuances and complexities that comprise the crisis. Passing legislation that solely addresses conflict minerals is an action that only treats a symptom of the problem. Even if the trade of conflict minerals was stopped, it is highly unlikely that all violence in the Congo would accordingly cease (Wolfe, 2015). The bottom line is that even if armed groups aren't fighting over minerals, there will always be something else to fight over. This is because conflict minerals were never the only source of conflict. The issues at play are political, ethnic, national, historical, and regional; they are issues of citizenship, of identity, of access to land (Raghavan, 2014). These are the significant drivers of conflict. These are the sorts of issues that should be considered and targeted in sanctions and legislation. The global understanding of the crisis in the Congo needs to be deepened and complicated because the problem is much greater and encompassing than the trade of conflict minerals, and understanding its intricacies is a vital component in being able to craft effective peace solutions. After all, how can legislators create a solution for a problem they do not fully understand?

Another aspect of foreign policy relating to the DRC that should be reconsidered is the practicality of any measures passed—that is, whether or not the laws can actually be carried out and enforced—particularly in regards to the conflict mineral trade (*An Open Letter*, 2014). Laws need to be realistic and feasible. Due diligence laws, while good enough in theory, are neither of these in practice. Such laws placed the brunt of the mineral certification process on the DRC itself, when the reality of the situation is that the DRC simply was not capable of bearing these responsibilities (Anderson, 2014). Advocates of laws like the Dodd-Frank Act expected the Congolese government to provide an environment for businesses in which they could produce due diligence reports and legitimately purchase minerals, but the mechanisms to do so did not and do not exist in the Congo, where there is still too much instability and corruption. Reports have claimed that as of 2010, there were not any traceability or certification systems in the DRC that met the full requirements of due diligence laws (Anderson, 2014).

The question that follows is somewhat obvious. What is the point of passing legislation if it exists in an environment that is unable to enforce it? Was Section 1502 of the Dodd-Frank Act instated merely for appearances, so companies could pat themselves on the back for their good-doing while washing their hands free of the conflict? Due diligence laws may be effective if there were a means of implementation. But implementing such certification procedures and institutions would be a struggle for any country, let alone one with such vast territory and such a decentralized, weak federal government as the DRC (Anderson, 2014). Therefore, when legislators are creating processes for peace, they need to work with what they've got. Solutions can only be effective if they can be carried out. Legislators need to search for helpful actions that are possible given the current means of the Congo and reality of its economic, political, and social situations.

This idea goes hand-in-hand with the suggestion that legislators need to make an effort toward improved consultation with the Congolese government and improved communication with Congolese commu-

nities. Neither group was taken much into account in the passing of the Dodd-Frank Act and due diligence laws: "few local stakeholders have been included in on-going international policy-making, and as a result realities on the ground have not always been taken into account" (*An Open Letter*, 2014, p. 1). Congolese insight about local context and power structures, however, could have been an invaluable resource in terms of crafting feasible, appropriate peace solutions (*An Open Letter*, 2014).

Furthermore, communication with the Congolese would have better helped legislators predict how well the Dodd-Frank Act would or would not have been received and implemented, as well as what the act's fall-out would be. For instance, had legislators better understood the needs of local civilians, they might have realized that most miners had little incentive to help carry out mineral certification schemes, even if the measures to do so were in place. Christoph Vogel, co-author of the aforementioned open letter about anti-conflict mineral legislation, explains that, "a Congolese miner has a lot of difficulty understanding the usefulness of these kinds of systems because for him or her the main thing is to earn a few bucks a day just to nourish their families" (Anderson, 2014). Had legislators grasped this mentality, they might have been better able to craft incentives for Congolese to cooperate with due diligence laws. Vogel, for instance, suggests incentives via improved business practices: "the more you can help them improve labor security in the mines and create better infrastructure, the more you will motivate them to become interested in these clean mineral frameworks" (Anderson, 2014).

This relates to other suggestions to use better business practices as incentives for legal mining activity. One suggestion, put forth in the open letter, is the imposition of a minimum wage to help curb corruption. Many Congolese default to black markets, tax fraud, and other illegal activities out of the need to provide and survive, since most are underpaid (*An Open Letter*, 2014). However, even this suggestion is not without its faults: if the Congolese government could not help enforce due diligence laws, will they really be able to enforce a minimum wage? The open letter also suggests the promotion of fair competition by giving miners increased leverage on price in the global arena and not underselling minerals, which may help standardize, equalize, and legalize the mineral trade (*An Open Letter*, 2014).

Another change that should be made at the legislative level is the push toward meaningful reform. This means that legislators need to critically and consciously be aware of who they are creating laws for and what their motives are. Take the Dodd-Frank Act, for example. It is, essentially, a piece of legislation that was created via Western framework and was then slapped on a very non-Western country that was frankly incompatible with the ideas and actions proposed in the Act. Considering this, one may ask: who was the Dodd-Frank Act for? Was it truly for the Congolese, as it claimed, or was it for the American people themselves? Consider this: the Dodd-Frank Act helped produce ethical goods for American consumers so that they could have clear consciences and peace of mind without having to sacrifice their iPhones, computers, televisions, and cars. At the same time, the Dodd-Frank Act did very little to improve the daily lives of the Congolese people, and in some instances, further damaged life in the Congo. Ultimately, it was a piece of legislation that benefited the consumers more than it benefited the producers (Gallo, 2011).

So, who was the Dodd-Frank Act for? Considering the above fall-out of the law, it seems as though it was very much oriented toward the satisfaction of the Americans and not the Congolese. It may even hint towards a bit of "white man's burden," echoing the Congo's past of manipulative imperialism—such as when Leopold plundered the DRC's resources, intervened in Congolese affairs, and ultimately hurt the country under the guise of helping the Africans. If legislators want to truly help in the Congo, then they need to set goals for meaningful reform for the day-to-day lives of the Congolese, not the appeasement of Western consumers. They need to make sure that the measures they are implementing are measures that are actually going to help the people that need help.

CONCLUSION

The Dodd-Frank Act and other anti-conflict mineral legislation were created with good intentions. Nevertheless, most legislation still failed to bring about conflict resolution in the DRC, and some even encouraged greater economic failure and thus increased conflict. The problem, then, is not necessarily with getting global legislators on board with the idea of helping the Congo find peace. Rather, the issue at hand is getting legislators to find the *right* ways to go about conflict resolution via trade and foreign policy.

Due diligence laws failed the DRC for a variety of reasons. They encouraged multinational businesses to pull out of Congolese investment, they were inefficient and ineffective as a result of turbulence in the DRC, and perhaps most importantly, they failed to address the roots of conflict in the Congo. If legislators want to truly help solve the crisis in the DRC, they need to achieve an understanding of why these measures failed and learn from their mistakes. They need to pass legislation with a full understanding of the complex causes of conflict, they need to customize conflict resolution measures so that they are compatible with the reality of the Congo's capabilities, and they need to use critical foresight to ensure that they are truly helping, not hurting, the people most in need of aid.

That being said, it is not solely the responsibility of international consumers and legislators to help the Congo find peace. Foreign policy and global sanctions can only do so much. If the DRC wants to have any true chance of attaining peace and stability, it needs to learn to help itself. Governmental reform is essential. The DRC needs a strong, centralized federal government that will be able to assert its authority over the various armed groups and feuding ethnicities in order to bring peace and unity to the region. Additionally, the government needs to crack down on corruption and increase transparency, or else the historical pattern of chaos and turmoil in Congolese politics will continue.

It is easy to call for the DRC to seek change, but whether or not the nation will actually be able to self-reform is another matter. If history does indeed repeat itself, then it seems that the Congo has a long road ahead of political, ethnic, and social disputes, of violence and corruption, and of international relations that usually do more harm than good. And there are plenty of people that do in fact think the Congo has passed the tipping point of salvation. One *National Geographic* article quoted a UN specialist who had been working on-site in the Congo for years: "There's no easy solution. I'm not even sure there is any solution" (Gettleman, 2013).

While it may be a bit too pessimistic and irrevocable to claim that there is no solution for the Congo, this UN specialist is right: there's no easy fix, there's no panacea for problems in the DRC. This is because there's nothing easy about the problems themselves. Conflict in the Congo stems from a complicated snarl of political tensions, corrupt transactions, severe poverty, ethnic divisions, problematic historical precedents, a culture of violence, and so much more. With so many issues to address, the Congo is going to need more than one solution. In fact, the DRC is going to need a groundswell of solutions—enough to assert a formidable presence in the Congo that sets a precedent for peace—because a few resolutions here and there are not going to amount to change on a national level, and "none of them has a realistic chance of success in isolation" (De Koning, 2011, p. 1).

With the massive nature of conflict in the Congo, it is going to take an accumulation of all of these things—foreign policy, Congolese self-reform, customized solutions in bulk—in order to see true change. Although the Dodd-Frank Act and anti-conflict mineral legislation did not bring about desired change, this does not mean the global community should give up on the Congo. After all, it was the international demand for resources in the DRC that created a pattern of extraction, violence, conflict, and instability, and it was the complex interconnections of globalization that helped create the conflict mineral trade and sustain the violence (De Koning, 2011). Global consumers are therefore implicated in conflict in the Congo, and as such it could be argued that it is a matter of global responsibility—perhaps even one of responsibility to protect—that makes the international community accountable for helping the Congo find peace.

While anti-conflict mineral legislation may not have resulted in its intended outcomes, the intentions behind the legislation were a good start. Conflict minerals may not be the root cause of problems in the Congo, but they are still a problem, and the global community was not wrong in trying to stop their trade. Hopefully, the failure of anti-conflict mineral legislation will not discourage foreign actors from pursuing peace efforts in the DRC. The shortcomings and negative fall-out of the Dodd-Frank Act and other anti-conflict mineral legislation should not be in vain. Instead, legislators should try to learn from their faults in order to produce stronger, more effective conflict resolutions, and should use the lessons learned from this failure as motivation to keep chasing peace in the DRC despite all the many obstacles that will come their way.

REFERENCES

Anderson, M. (2014, September 10). DR Congo's miners bear brunt of attempts to make minerals conflict-free. *The Guardian.* Retrieved from http://gu.com/p/4xdng/stw

Arieff, A. (2014). Democratic Republic of Congo: Background and U.S. policy. *Current Politics and Economics of Africa, 7*(2), 113-142.

Arnaud, C. H. (2012). Fingerprinting conflict minerals. *Chemical and Engineering News, 90*(18), 36-37.

BBC. (2015, August 4). Democratic Republic of Congo profile: Timeline. (2015, August 4). *BBC News.* Retrieved from http://www.bbc.com/news/world-africa-13286306

Business Monitor International. (2014). *Congo, Dem. Rep. mining report Q1 2015.* London, England: Business Monitor International.

Collier, P. (2010). The political economy of natural resources. *Social Research: An International Quarterly, 77*(4), 1105-1132.

Collier, P. & Hoeffler, A. (2004). Greed and grievance in civil war. *Oxford Economic Papers, 56*(4), 563-595. doi:10.1093/oep/gpf064

De Koning, R. (2011). *Conflict minerals in the Democratic Republic of Congo: Aligning trade and security interventions.* Solna, Sweden: Stockholm International Peace Research Institute. Retrieved from http://books.sipri.org/files/PP/SIPRIPP27.pdf

Dodd-Frank Wall Street Reform and Consumer Protection Act, 111 U.S.C. § 1502 et seq. (2010).

Drajem, M., Hamilton, J. & Kavanagh, M. J. (2011, August 4). A rule aimed at warlords upends African mines. *Bloomberg Business*. Retrieved from http://www.bloomberg.com/bw/magazine/a-rule-aimed-at-warlords-upends-african-mines-08042011.html

Engineering and Mining Journal. (2000). Current status of mining in the Democratic Republic of Congo. *Engineering and Mining Journal, 201*(5), 20-26.

Gallo, C. J. (2011, August 9). Digging deeper into the Dodd-Frank Congo 'blood minerals' controversy. *UN Dispatch*. Retrieved from http://go.shr.lc/1MTxWKl

Gettleman, J. (2013, October). The price of precious. *National Geographic*. Retrieved from http://ngm.nationalgeographic.com/2013/10/conflict-minerals/gettleman-text

Gondola, C. D. (2002). *The history of Congo*. Westport, CT: Greenwood Publishing Group.

Haskin, J. M. (2005). *The tragic state of the Congo: From decolonization to dictatorship*. New York, NY: Algora Publishing.

International Peace Information Service. (2013). *The formalisation of artisanal mining in the Democratic Republic of the Congo and Rwanda*. Retrieved from http://www.cifor.org/fileadmin/subsites/proformal/PDF/RIPIS1212.pdf

KPMG Global Mining Institute. (2014). *Democratic Republic of Congo: Country mining guide*. Amsterdam, Netherlands: KPMG International Cooperative. Retrieved from https://assets.kpmg.com/content/dam/kpmg/pdf/2014/09/democratic-republic-congo-mining-guide.pdf

Lecomte, V. (2015). The Kimberley Process: A new actor on the conflict resolution scene? [Undergraduate research]. Lund, Sweden: Lund University, Department of Political Science. Retrieved from https://lup.lub.lu.se/student-papers/search/publication/4925566

Lee, P. (2010, March 11). China has a Congo copper headache. *Asia Times*. Retrieved from http://www.atimes.com/atimes/China_Business/LC11Cb02.html

Nanda, V. P. (2014). Conflict minerals and international business: United States and international responses. *ILSA Journal of International & Comparative Law, 20*(2), 285-304.

Natural Resource Governance Institute. (n.d.). *Dem. Rep. of Congo*. Retrieved from http://www.resourcegovernance.org/countries/africa/democratic-republic-congo/overview

An open letter. (2014). Retrieved from https://ethuin.files.wordpress.com/2014/09/09092014-open-letter-final-and-list.pdf

Organisation for Economic Cooperation and Development. (2013). *OECD due diligence guidance for responsible supply chains of minerals from conflict-affected and high-risk areas* (2nd ed.). Paris, France: OECD Publishing. doi:10.1787/9789264185050-en

Propper, S. & Knight, P. (2013, December 4). 'Conflict free' minerals from the DRC will only be possible if companies stay. *The Guardian*. Retrieved from http://gu.com/p/3yvc4/stw

Raghavan, S. (2014, November 30). How a well-intentioned U.S. law left Congolese miners jobless. *Washington Post*. Retrieved from http://wapo.st/1ya3bbt?

Raj, S. (2011). Blood electronics: Congo's conflict minerals and the legislation that could cleanse the trade. *Southern California Law Review 84*(4), 981-1034.

Reno, W. (2007). Patronage politics and behavior of armed groups. *Civil Wars, 9*(4), 324-342. doi:10.1080/13698240701699409

Rhode, D. (2014, March 24). The Kimberley Process is a perfect 'cover story' for blood diamonds. *The Guardian*. Retrieved from http://gu.com/p/3nyaq/stw

U.S. Geological Survey. (2015). *Mineral commodity summaries*. Washington, DC: U.S. Government Printing Office. doi:10.3133/70140094

Weissman, S. R. (1974). *American foreign policy in the Congo, 1960-1964*. Ithaca, NY: Cornell University Press.

Wigny, P. (1961). Belgium and the Congo. *International Affairs (Royal Institute of International Affairs 1944-), 37*(3), 273-284. doi:10.2307/2610922

Wolfe, L. (2015, February 2). How Dodd-Frank is failing Congo. *Foreign Policy.* Retrieved from http://foreignpolicy.com/2015/02/02/how-dodd-frank-is-failing-congo-mining-conflict-minerals/

Young, C. (1965). *Politics in the Congo: Decolonization and independence.* Princeton, NJ: Princeton University Press.

An Interview with Katherine A. Mannion

Hometown: *Stewart Manor, NY*

Major: *Communication*

Hobbies: *Knitting and reading.*

Do/did you like Geneseo? Why did you choose to come to Geneseo?

Katherine: I loved Geneseo! I was a member of the crew team, the college radio and worked for the Ice Knights while I attended, so I was really involved in some cool activities. I made some of the best friends I have ever had at Geneseo. Plus, you can't beat a Geneseo sunset!

I wanted to get the best education possible in the state system, and Geneseo was notorious for having exactly that. I also wanted to go away for school but still be in state and close enough that I could get home easily. Geneseo satisfied that desire for me.

Why do you feel that GREAT Day is important?

GREAT Day gives students an incredible opportunity to showcase their skills and research. Often the work that is being presented has been a project for most of the year, if not longer, and it allows students to show off work they have done that they are truly proud of. It also establishes Geneseo as a hot spot in the SUNY system for undergraduate research in a variety of different subject areas.

How did it feel to present your work at GREAT Day?

Presenting at GREAT Day was a fun experience. I loved being able to showcase my work to my professors, fellow students, and friends. It was incredibly rewarding to have a tangible presentation for the work that I did over the course of the academic year.

Play Like a Girl: An Analysis of Media Representation of Female Athletes

Katherine A. Mannion

ABSTRACT

This paper critically examines the relationship between media representation of female athletes and the public opinion of female athletes. Research has shown that female athletes are more likely to be sexualized than male athletes and are therefore delegitimized in their skill. Through analysis of sports websites and a survey distributed online through a midsized, public, liberal arts college in the Northeast, data was gathered to establish the public opinion of female athletes. Research presented shows that female athletes are delegitimized and sexualized as a result of a lack of proficient coverage of their athletic skills and pursuits.

Both the general public and the producers of sports media view women's sports in America as less important, less relevant, and less worthwhile than men's sports. This has led to problems, including a lack of representation in the media, a lack of places for young women to play sports professionally, a lack of female role models for female athletes, and dangerous playing conditions for female athletes. Investigating this problem will get to the root of the reasoning for and uncover the extent of this issue.

Previous research in the field has shown that women are not fairly represented in the media or on the playing field. Harris polls from the last three years have shown a lack of interest from the public in women's sports (Corso, 2014; Braverman, 2011), while data from 2009 shows that major networks like ESPN only gave 1.6% of their coverage to women's sports (Messner & Cooky, 2009). Other research has found that when young women do not see female athletes, they feel discouraged from participating and stop playing (Schmalz, 2006). It has also been shown that women are represented best in sports where their bodies can be sexualized and they can be shown off as being attractive (Hilliard, 1984). This study will investigate these claims, namely the extent of the lacking representation of female athletes and the effect it has on public perception of these athletes. This study hypothesizes that women's sports media representation is minimal, and that the public perception of female athletes is sexual and delegitimizes

their ability to perform. The research will include a comprehensive look at modern sports reporting and the opinions of young people on women's sports in order to find out if there is a relationship between the two. The study will discuss how sports media affects the way female athletes are perceived by the public.

This study will have practical implications in that it will uncover the issues in representation for women's sports in the media and in the eyes of the public. It will provide a springboard for the continuance of changes in the way women's sports are represented and how female athletes are perceived. It may provide a positive effect on young sports-playing women to encourage them to stay in the game.

LITERATURE REVIEW

Sports in America

In the United States, sports are a large part of the identity of the nation. According to a Harris poll, most Americans watch football (Braverman, 2011). Three quarters of men and over half of women watch somewhere between 1 and 16 hours of football per week, whether it is watching multiple games or participating in fantasy leagues (Braverman, 2011). A different Harris poll also found that a majority of Americans say professional football is their favorite sport in general, with 35% reporting as such (Corso, 2014). Professional baseball garnered 14% in a field of 21 options.

Sports as a cultural identity. The large role that sports play in the American culture shows how they construct the social identity of America. The creation of a cultural phenomenon has several aspects. Culture, first and foremost, is the way that humans organize themselves and create relatable ideas that have common ground across differences. Generally, film, music, and celebrities create culture. According to Lull (2000), culture is not just the existence of these things, but the way that the ideas, values, and things are reacted to, interpreted, and spread through communication. Therein, culture is both a source and a resource. It is a source in that it generates what is being reacted to and it is a resource in that it creates something for humans to react to and build an identity around. Culture is always changing, and the public opinion of certain aspects of culture can shift rapidly from positive to negative depending on how it is being presented.

Sports are a cultural phenomenon in that they are an obsession of the American people that occupies much of the nation's time and energy. They are also used as vehicles to promote teamwork, physical fitness, and hard work, as demonstrated by the different campaigns athletes participate in. For example, the "I Will What I Want" campaign from Under Armour® promotes enthusiasm for fitness and achieving goals, and features athletes including Kelley O'Hara, Misty Copeland, and Briana Cope. Michael Jordan was featured in the "Be Like Mike" campaign where he encouraged young people to become like him by drinking Gatorade. These athletes are figureheads and role models for values, and Americans adjust their views to match those of their favorite athletes.

This idea that athletes are role models and promote teamwork and other values is in part due to the cultivation theory, which posits that people will believe television reflects reality and adjust their views accordingly (Gerbner, 1976). Cultivation theory has been used as a cornerstone for the effects of media on consumers. Researchers have found that those who watch more television are more likely to be discontented because their lives do not resemble the world on television. Many studies have reflected that constant media consumption leads to poor psychological health and warped perceptions of reality (Dittmar, 1994; McCreary & Sadaca, 1999). The hypermasculine idea presented through sports media contributes to the hegemonic masculinity that promotes strength, power, and aggression as traits specifically for men.

Fanaticism associated with sports. The influence of sports culture on America is directly related to increased fanaticism, or relation and passion for a certain thing (Wang, 2006). Sports fanaticism has led to increased camaraderie amongst Americans. In *Signs of Life in the USA,* it is suggested that this camaraderie is due to a certain amount of escapism from everyday life that sports provide. According to Maasik and Solomon (1994), sports create a way for American men to remove themselves from the home, their jobs, and other benign activities and vigorously engage in watching or playing extreme physical sports. Wang (2006) posits that Americans use sports teams to identify themselves, similar to the way they identify with a race or geographical location. Americans use their favorite sports teams to create a community of people who are interested in the same things as themselves.

Fanaticism also has a darker side, creating more ways for hardcore fans to be aggressive, mean, and almost dangerous. Fanatics have a conviction that their understanding is absolutely right, which reflects in sports fans when they aggressively defend their favorite teams and athletes (Marimaa, 2011). Marimaa (2011) also states that fanatics try to push their allegiances onto others. This correlates with Wang's (2006) study, which states that fans of winning teams encourage others to also root for their team and will be crude, crass, and downright violent to those who disagree with them. Therefore, although the fanaticism brings Americans together in united excitement, it also creates tension when there are differing opinions. The fanaticism is primarily related to male sports, however, as male sports are seen as more aggressive and deserving of crazed obsession than women's. This obsession fuels the occupation Americans have with men's sports that involves aggression and forms the public's opinion.

Gender in Sports

The Harris poll asking for the favorite sports of the participants has been taken annually since 1985 (Corso, 2014). Sports played by women were not included in the poll questions until 2000. However, when they were included in the survey they consistently ranked low, earning less than 0.5% of the votes every year, with the exception of women's tennis and women's college basketball, which pulled 1% of the votes in a few different years (Corso, 2014). Traditional gender roles and heteronormativity may play a role in the distaste the American public has for women's sports (Schmalz, 2006; Greendorfer, 1987).

Sports are often seen as hypermasculine physical events. By merely participating in certain sports that are seen as not "appropriate," people send messages to the people around them about certain characteristics (Messner, 2002). When asked to distinguish girls' sports from boys' sports, young girls had more difficulty explaining why certain sports, like baseball, did not include women, while boys were content explaining that girls should not become dirty so they cannot play football and boys should not wave their hands in a certain way so they cannot cheerlead (Schmalz, 2006). According to Schmalz's (2006) study, data collected from interviewing young people showed that women are more likely to play more masculine sports at a young age than men are likely to play feminine sports. Additionally, a Women's Sports Foundation Study states that girls who participate in sports and receive positive reinforcement in their youth are more likely to continue to play into adulthood, casually or professionally (Greendorfer, 1987). However, young girls are highly likely to face strict scrutiny as they grow up and continue playing their sport.

While Title IX requires that girls in school be offered the same opportunities to participate in sports as boys, according to Yu (1993), literature presented to children appears to do the opposite, showing young girls playing sports in picture books only about 25% of the time (Yu, 1993). This underlying sexism creates an environment that enforces gender roles, establishing men as more likely to continue playing sports and excel than women. So although women are more likely to play masculine sports as young people, they are likely to stop as adults as they are told to grow out of it.

Trujillo (1991) argues that sports culture is a result of hegemonic masculinity. Hegemonic masculinity is created as a result of physical force and dominance. Therefore, when men play sports and place themselves above women as dominant, powerful forces, they reinforce traditional roles and the patriarchy. According to Trujillo's (1991) study, masculinity is enforced by the dominant group's claims that sports create a hypermasculine society. Football especially emphasizes sanctioned aggression and violence. The banning of women from this sport reinforces patriarchal values that women are weak and unable to be as strong as men.

Women's Sports

Evolution of women's sports in America. Sports are considered a largely male-dominated space. The "big four" major league sports—baseball, football, basketball, and hockey—expressly prohibit women from playing, but did not always. According to several *New York Times* reports, a female pitcher contracted with an AA team by the name of Jackie Mitchell struck out both Lou Gehrig and Babe Ruth during an exhibition game (Brandt, W. E., 1931). A fear that the mound would become feminine led to her contract being voided. Women were formally banned from baseball in 1952 because it was considered by Commissioner Kenesaw Landis to be "too strenuous" for women (as cited in Pietrusza, 1998, p. 374). While there is no explicit rule in either rulebook, neither the NHL nor the NFL have ever accepted female players onto teams. Due to this, women have been forced to create their own leagues.

Historically, while there have been several attempts to form and operate women's professional sports leagues, they do not succeed when compared to men's professional leagues. Softball, considered a safe alternative to baseball, existed as the International Women's Professional Softball Association, or IWPSA, until 1980. The league folded due to a fiscal difficulty and in 1982 the NCAA began to sponsor college softball. This allowed the U.S. Women's National Softball team to form, and after several victories on the international stage, enough professional sponsors finally came together to create the WPSL, or Women's Professional Softball League. They have since changed their name to National Fastpitch Softball, according to their website. Women's hockey formed a professional league in 1999 that lasted only eight years (NWHL, n.d.). There is currently no single professional women's hockey league in America even though the U.S. Women's National Hockey team holds medals from the last five Winter Olympic

Games (USA Hockey, n.d.). Female sports leagues seem unable to thrive, as seen here, possibly because women's ability to play their sports is considered to be less valuable than a man's.

Why women's sports are not valued. According to Messner (1988), increasing athleticism in women does not signal increased freedom for women within sports. The attempts of women throughout history to overcome the bounds of hegemonic masculinity have been aggressively shut down by those in power. Female athletes have historically had to define their beauty by the standards put forth by men. The only movement to contest this was the women's body-building movement, which allowed women to define what was strongest and "best" (Messner, 1988). Men respond to women who excel in athletics by stating that they would not do well if they were in a man's version of the sport. Hegemonic masculinity is so ingrained in culture that the media uses its coverage to align American values with male sports, and with other females playing sports that are considered to be more masculine.

Media coverage of women's sports. As media has become the primary way to watch, judge, and analyze sports, coverage of sports news has become almost entirely male-focused. In an observation of the 1992 Olympics done by Higgs and Weiller (2003), they found that when reporters covered women's sports, they covered them by using degrading comments about the female athletes' bodies and physiques instead of judging their ability to participate in their respective sports. Words including "strong" and "aggressive" were used to describe male athletes nearly 3 times as often as they were for women (Higgs & Weiller, 2003). It was also found in the next three sets of Olympic Games that sports media conglomerates claimed to promote equal opportunities for female and male coverage, but overhyped male sports and barely promoted female sports (Higgs & Weiller, 2003). The female sports that were promoted were ones men found aesthetically pleasing, such as gymnastics and swimming (Riebock, 2012).

In addition to Olympic coverage, bias exists during the regular season as well. In 2011, the Badminton World Federation demanded that all female players wear short skirts in order to make play more appealing to viewers. The rule was considered not only to be sexist, but disrespectful to players whose religious ideologies prevented them from being able to wear short skirts. It was publicly decried as sexist and was eventually overturned, but remained in place long enough to anger professional female athletes both inside and outside of the sport (Longman, 2011).

A prime example of poorly covered female athletes is the United States Women's National Soccer Team. This team is one of the premier women's teams in the world. It has won five Olympic gold medals and has medaled at every Olympic Games it has attended since 1996. It has also won the Gold Cup at the Confederation of North, Central American, and Caribbean Association Football (CONCACAF) tournament six times. The Women's National team has also placed at the World Cup every time they have competed since 1991, winning twice. They brought America's attention back to the sport in 2012 after winning a gold medal at the Olympics and were able to create an American league for the regular season. However, they are subjected to sexism in the media and within their own sport. They are rarely presented in athletic poses in magazines, a common trend amongst female athletes, and they have made the cover of *Sports Illustrated* a total of three times (Wahl, 2014), once for sportswoman of the year.

Underlying sexism can be found even within the organizations that fund women's sports. After examining the FIFA website, it has been found that the group values men's soccer over women's (Meân, 2010). The FIFA website's top stories were 97.3% on men's soccer and the stories were severely lacking in terms of results for World Cup Qualifiers, which occurred at the time of the story (Meân, 2010). Additionally, photographs of athletes on the site were mostly of men, but the few photographs of women showed the women from the waist up, celebrating their success or hugging their teammates instead of actually participating in the sport (Meân, 2010). Lack of representation within the organization that runs the event shows the underlying sexism within the sport. Not identifying, glorifying, or heralding female athletes for doing the same work that the male athletes do classifies them as "others" and diminishes their worth as athletes.

Female soccer players' ability to play their sport is inhibited by sexist rules put in place by their federations. FIFA has announced a bid to play the Women's World Cup on turf instead of grass. This is considered dangerous, and has been called "padded concrete" by Women's National Team player Megan Rapinoe (Peterson, 2014). It is more likely to cause injury and prevents playing the game to the fullest for fear of injury, according to a recent study (Sousa, Rebelo, & Brito, 2013). More than half of the participants in this study were injured on turf during their season as a direct result of the turf field (Sousa et al., 2013). Abby Wambach and 40 other international players have filed a lawsuit against FIFA for discriminating against them according to Canadian and international statutes, alleging that playing on turf creates danger and is a violation of human rights laws in that it denies female players the right to play on the same level as male players (Dellinger, 2014). Women are expected to have the same opportunities that men have on the field and playing on turf prevents that.

METHODS

The research gained from this study will principally be used to examine the phenomenon of misrepresentation or lack of representation of female athletes in sports and sports media. Using data from the study, conclusions will be drawn regarding the public perception of female athletes. Principally, the study will focus on how people who either follow or do not follow sports see women's sports compared to the amount of representation within the media. The study will also look at the sexualization of female athletes by major sports outlets both on and off their respective fields, with a focus on women's soccer. By looking at this information specifically, it is hoped that a root for the cause of the discrimination, as well as the public perception of the discrimination's extent, can be found.

Website Analysis

In conducting this study, sports media conglomerates and their coverage's breadth will be analyzed first. ESPN, Fox Sports, and BleacherReport will be the focus of the study. These conglomerates are the best-known sports programs on the national level and set the bar for local sports reports (Tuggle, 2009). The study was done by viewing the websites for each sports conglomerate and comparing the amount of time given to women's sports and to men's sports. In

a 2009 study looking at similar factors, it was found that women's sports received 1.6% of the coverage in major sports shows, while men's sports received 96.3% of the coverage (Messner & Cooky, 2009).

Survey

A final method of this research study was an analysis of public opinion on the coverage of women's sports in the media. This was done using a survey distributed through Google Forms. The survey had about 20 questions and took somewhere between 5 and 10 minutes to complete. The population to be evaluated was that of a liberal arts college in the northeastern region of the United States. The college has approximately 5,000 students and is located in a rural area with approximately 30,000 people in it from backgrounds varying from metropolitan to rural to international, allowing for a broad range of responses. Additionally, the college has a history of fairly successful athletic programs. Respondents were asked about their interest level in sports as well as their ability to name female athletes and sports leagues.

A similar study to this one was conducted with middle school boys as subjects by showing the subjects athletes and models in several positions and evaluating their reactions. The students were presented with 15 pictures of white women and asked for their opinions (Daniels & Wartena, 2011). The study found that sexualized athletes were written about more for their appearance, alignment with the female ideal, and sexuality than performance athletes were (Daniels & Wartena, 2011). This study will perform a similar experiment. The researcher will show members of the focus group photographs of athletes in two different positions, sexualized and in action. The subjects will then be asked for three adjectives to describe both images of athletes. From there, data will be put together about how athletes are viewed in different scenarios. The athletes were chosen based on whether or not they had photographs in the ESPN Body Issue.

ANALYSIS

Website Results

On the ESPN website's home page there were 43 stories featured across a broad range of sports, including college and major league athletics. Because of the time of year, most of the stories were about college and national football, as well as college basketball. Of these 43 stories, one was about a female athlete. Statistically speaking, this is approximately 2% of stories. This story linked to the website ESPNW, the ESPN site dedicated to women, and was about Heather Hardy, a female boxer. However, the article did not focus on her wins or athletic prowess but rather on the hardships she has faced as a female boxer. It discussed her selling tickets to her own fights and being sexually assaulted by a coach (Larriva, 2014). It repeatedly emphasized her flaws, and even went as far as to say "she isn't the best or smartest fighter out there" in an article meant to herald her strengths (Larriva, 2014). In fact, the article repeatedly emphasized the fact that boxing is not ready for an all-female card.

Bleacher Report, another sports conglomerate, had no female athletes or women's sports on their main web page. In their top 10 stories, two were about football, two were about basketball, two were about hockey, and the other four were public interest stories, including an athlete's new line of sneakers and a "kiss cam" mishap. None of the stories were about women's sports. At the bottom of the home page for the site, a list of 10 "featured authors" in varying sports was listed. One of these authors was female. Additionally, the website provided tabs that users could hover over to select teams. Even though these sports included college basketball, mixed martial arts fighting, and hockey, no women's leagues or teams were available to select. There was also no link for a separate website dedicated to women's sports.

A final website, Fox Sports, also had no female sports stories on their front page. There was one story about Danica Patrick, but not in the context of her sport. It highlighted her attending a country music awards show. The story did not contain any reporting but was a slideshow of her posing with different country musicians on the red carpet for the event. While Danica Patrick is a high-profile auto racer within the sport of NASCAR, the article was about her in terms of fashion at an award show unrelated to NASCAR. Within the story, Danica Patrick was introduced as a GoDaddy.com representative before a NASCAR racer. GoDaddy is a company that uses sexualized images of women to sell website domains. Finally, a sidebar containing most recent sports scores, titled "All Sports," did not contain any female sports scores, despite covering college soccer and hockey.

Image Analysis

In a survey distributed through Google Forms, there were 193 respondents. The survey was open to people with email addresses for the college surveyed. Survey respondents were predominantly female, with 75% of the respondents reporting as such. Sixty-eight percent of the respondents said they had considered themselves athletes at some point in their lives, and 69% said they follow sports. Football is the most followed sport, followed closely by baseball and hockey Research participants were presented with images of three female athletes and three male athletes in two different poses. One set of images was from the Body Issue of *ESPN Magazine* and the other set were the athletes playing their respective sports. Participants were asked to give three adjectives to describe their opinion of the athletes based solely on the images. The six athletes all received distinct opinions from each other.

Male images. The male images were of Marshawn Lynch, a professional football player; Michael Phelps, a swimmer; and Prince Fielder, a professional baseball player. These three men were shown mostly naked in one image and seen playing their respective sports in the second image. Marshawn Lynch was shown in a lunging position, naked, holding a football in his Body Issue picture. Michael Phelps was shown lunging from a diving block presumably towards the water. Prince Fielder is shown holding a baseball bat behind his head and turned to the side. Their action shots are Marshawn Lynch in full gear setting up a play, Michael Phelps swimming freestyle, and Prince Fielder swinging at a pitch.

For Lynch, the most common word given as a response (62.9% of the time) was "strong." Second to this was the word "muscular," given as a response 58% of the time. Many participants stated that Lynch's pictures made him look tough and threatening, as well as "committed," "proud," and "ambitious." Often, participants would use the word "threatening" in addition to a positive adjective. The most-used adjective for Phelps was "muscular," appearing 27% of the time. "Strong" appeared in 17% of responses. Respondents were also apt to mention his drug use, which could not be gathered from the images and might have tainted results. Prince Fielder, who is notably heavier and less defined than either of these athletes, received responses with different connotations. While the predominant adjective given was "strong" (28%), 25% of respondents used some variation of the words "fat," "heavy," or "overweight" when describing him.

Female images. The female images were of Alex Morgan, a professional soccer player; Miesha Tate, a professional mixed martial arts fighter; and Hilary Knight, a professional hockey player. As with the men, in one image the women were shown mostly naked in various positions and in the other they were in action. Alex Morgan's first image is her lying on a beach in a prone position, wet presumably from the water. Miesha Tate's is her wearing only pink hand wraps and covering her breasts. Hilary Knight is wearing nothing but hockey skates and surrounded by hockey equipment, bending over as to hide her breasts. In Morgan's second picture she is receiving a pass, in Tate's she is kicking an opponent, and in Knight's she is executing a shot.

The most prevalent word for Alex Morgan was "athletic," with 33% of respondents using it. However, 36% of respondents used words to objectify and sexualize. These words include "hot," "sexy," "beautiful," and "attractive." Additionally, the word "strong" was used just as often as the word "sexy" by 16.2% of respondents. Miesha Tate's adjectives most closely resembled those commonly used for the male athletes. Forty-seven percent of respondents used the word "strong" to describe her; 21% of respondents used sexual language to describe her, including words like "sexy," "hot," and "beautiful;" 33% of respondents called Hilary Knight "strong," and 17% called her "athletic;" and finally, 52% of respondents used sexual language to describe her, including "sexy," "attractive," "pretty," "hot," and "gorgeous."

Websites lacked coverage. The websites rarely, if ever, had stories about female athletes. This result is not surprising and is supported by the study by Higgs and Weiller (2003) that found sports networks often failed to give equal media time to women's sports. Additionally, the few sports stories that did cover women's sports appeared to objectify the women. Heather Hardy's story discussed her in terms of her lack of skill instead of the skill she definitely has (Larriva, 2014). The women's sports covered were also usually aesthetically pleasing sports or related to events outside of the sport that were focused on aesthetics. An example of this is the coverage of Danica Patrick. While she manages to hold a high position in a male-dominated sport, she is sexualized and fetishized as a result of hegemonic masculinity. As shown in the only women's sports story on the Fox Sports site, Patrick is delegitimized by being sexualized in order to keep her from overshadowing men she surpasses in skill.

Expected results. Examining the words used by participants to describe the athletes led to expected results. While both men and women were described as "strong" across the board, certain athletes were more likely to receive that descriptor than others. Marshawn Lynch was overwhelmingly called "strong," and Hilary Knight was also often described as "strong." The key similarity between the two of them is the muscle definition in their naked pictures. However, Lynch received few descriptors sexualizing him. Knight's strength was often coupled with her sexual appeal or beauty. While the descriptors used for all of the athletes were fairly similar, and almost entirely complimentary, female athletes were sexualized when the male athletes were not. Female-typed words such as "fierce" or "fit" were used more often than words like "tough." These differing explanations for athletes of similar fitness levels in similar positions strengthens the idea that hegemonic masculinity adds more value to males than females in terms of their athleticism.

DISCUSSION AND CONCLUSION

This study highlights and examines the media coverage of female athletes as well as the public's opinion of the presentation of female athletes. The study identifies the difference in narrative between male athletes and female athletes both in the media and in the public eye. The presentation of female athletes on sports websites compared to the words used to describe female athletes shows a clear "othering" within the genre. While men are constantly called "strong," women are often called "fit" or identified using sexual or female-typed words. Men do not receive any praise in terms of their physical appearance outside of outright athleticism.

This study supports and adds to the work of Higgs and Weiller (2003), who noted that reporters were more likely to discuss the physical appearance of female athletes in terms of attractiveness than their athletic abilities. The statistics gained from the research participants in this study support Higgs and Weiller's (2003) work closely, showing that a male-typed word ("strong") was used 4 times more often for male athletes than for female athletes (62.9% to 16%), whereas female-typed words like "fit" and "fierce" were exclusively used for female athletes. Additionally, Daniels and Wartena's (2011) study found that high school boys were more likely to discuss the body types and appearance of female athletes when the athletes were shown in passive poses rather than in their in-action poses. The present study suggests that people, in this case people between the ages of 18 and 25, will sexualize female athletes if presented with a provocative image, even if the image is side by side with an action shot.

Along with female-typed words, female images are often passively posed. Goffman's (1979) concept of the feminine touch states that women are more likely to pose cradling things instead of carrying them in order to seem more passive. For example, in the image presented to the focus group of Hilary Knight, she is surrounded by hockey gear but not holding or wearing any of it, and bent over as if reaching for her skates. In the action image, she is tightly gripping her hockey stick and intensely focused. Goffman (1979) also posits that women are often photographed as distant and drifting from the scene. Photographs of Alex Morgan and Meisha Tate show them staring into the distance and not focused on the camera, dehumanizing them and allowing them to be sexualized further.

The lack of coverage of female athletes in action solidifies the hypermasculinity of the sports world and the ease through which they are sexualized. News outlets not covering female athletes for their achievements establish men as the superior athletes and delegitimize women's participation in sports in general. As mentioned earlier, young women who do not see athletes in action are less likely to continue playing sports (Yu, 1993). Additionally, when women are shown in sports media, they are shown out of the context of their performance, as evidenced by ESPN's story about Heather Hardy and her struggles to become a boxer rather than her achievements as a boxer. When athletes are not shown participating in their sports, it makes it difficult for the general public to see them as athletes and not just sexual beings.

When asked to name female athletes, participants mentioned the same four athletes repeatedly, all of whom broke into a traditionally male sport or had some sort of scandal surrounding them. Serena Williams and Venus Williams have dominated the game of tennis and won repeatedly but have also been surrounded by scandals, including being accused of being too masculine by the head of the Russian Tennis Federation ("Russian Official Not Sorry," 2014). Hope Solo has been successful as a soccer goalie but also has been surrounded by domestic abuse scandals (Sullivan, 2014). As the analysis of websites showed, female athletes are often not written about for their skills in games but for outside events such as attending festivals or struggling in their home lives. This study reinforces the claim that a lack of serious coverage of sports delegitimizes the women who play them and creates images of sexuality and weakness.

This study's examination of media coverage and public opinion sheds a bit of light on the general trends of misogyny within the sports world. Further research could continue to create a link between the coverage, or lack thereof, of female sports and the way athletes are viewed in the public sphere. Although female athletes are continuing to achieve and becoming more recognizable in the public eye, there is more to be done to ensure female athletes are recognized for athletic prowess and that young girls are encouraged to play sports by seeing people like themselves succeeding. Researching this topic further could help change trends of misogyny and "othering" within the sports world and create a more equal environment.

REFERENCES

Bishop, R. (2003). Missing in action: Feature coverage of women's sports in Sports Illustrated. *Journal of Sport & Social Issues, 27*(2), 184-194. doi:10.1177/0193732502250718

Brandt, W. E. (1931, April 3). Girl pitcher fans Ruth and Cehrig. *The New York Times*, p. 29.

Braverman, S. (2011, October 14). America's sport: A majority of Americans watch NFL football. *The Harris Poll.* Retrieved from http://www.theharrispoll.com/sports/America_s_Sport_A_Majority_of_Americans_Watch_NFL_Football.html

Corso, R. A. (2014, January 16). As American as mom, apple pie, and football? Football continues to be America's favorite sport. *The Harris Poll.* Retrieved from http://www.theharrispoll.com/sports/As_American_as_Mom__Apple_Pie_and_Football__.html

Daniels, E. A., & Wartena, H. (2011). Athlete or sex symbol: What boys think of media representations of female athletes. *Sex Roles, 65*(7-8), 566–579. doi:10.1007/s11199-011-9959-7

Dellinger, H. (2014, September 23). *RE: Final notice before players are forced to initiate legal action* [Personal communication and draft legal brief]. Retrieved from http://assets.espn.go.com/pdf/2014/0926/csafifa_final-notice.pdf

Dittmar, M. L. (1994). Relationship between depression, gender, and television viewing of college students. *Journal of Social Behavior and Personality, 9*(2), 317-328.

Edwards, L., & Jones, C. (2009). Postmodernism, queer theory, and moral judgement in sport: Some critical reflections. *International Review for the Sociology of Sport, 44*(4), 331-344. doi:10.1177/1012690209346082

Gerbner, G., & Gross, L. (1976). Living with television: The violence profile. *Journal of Communication, 26*(2), 172-194. doi:10.1111/j.1460-2466.1976.tb01397.x

Greendorfer, S. L. (1987). Gender bias in theoretical perspectives. *Psychology of Women Quarterly, 11*(3), 327-340. doi:10.1111/j.1471-6402.1987.tb00907.x

Hammermeister, J., Brock, B., Winterstein, D., & Page, R. (2005). Life without TV? Cultivation theory and psychosocial health characteristics of television-free individuals and their television-viewing counterparts. *Health Communication, 17*(3), 253-264. doi:10.1207/s15327027hc1703_3

Higgs, C. T., & Weiller, K. H. (1994). Gender bias and the 1992 Summer Olympic Games: An analysis of television coverage. *Journal of Sport & Social Issues, 18*(3), 234-246. doi:10.1177/019372394018003004

Hilliard, D. C. (1984). Media images of male and female professional athletes: An interpretive analysis of magazine articles. *Sociology of Sport Journal, 1*(3), 251-262.

Larriva, S. (2014, December 3). Why you should root for rising boxing star Heather Hardy. *ESPNW.* Retrieved from http://espn.go.com/espnw/news-commentary/article/11970844/why-root-rising-boxing-star-heather-hardy

Longman, J. (2011, May 26). Badminton's new dress code is being criticized for being sexist. *The New York Times.* Retrieved from http://nyti.ms/M1GprW

Lull, J. (2000). *Media, communication, culture: A global approach* (2nd ed.). New York, NY: Columbia University Press.

Maasik, S., & Solomon, J. (1994). *Signs of life in the USA.* Boston, MA: Bedford Books of St. Martin's Press.

Marimaa, K. (2011). The many faces of fanaticism. *ENDC Proceedings, 14*, 29-55.

Meân, L. J. (2010). Making masculinity and framing femininity: FIFA, soccer, and World Cup web sites. In H. Hundley & A. Billings (Eds.), *Examining identity in sports media* (pp. 1-15). Thousand Oaks, CA: Sage Publications.

McCreary, D., & Sadaca, S (1999). Television viewing and self-perceived health, weight, and physical fitness: Evidence for the cultivation hypothesis. *Journal of Applied Social Psychology, 29*, 2342-2361. doi:10.1111/j.1559-1816.1999.tb00114.x

Messner, M. A. (2002). *Taking the field: Women, men, and sports.* Minneapolis, MN: University of Minnesota Press.

Messner, M. A., & Cooky, C. (2010). *Gender in televised sports: News and highlight shows, 1989–2009.* Retrieved from https://dornsifecms.usc.edu/assets/sites/80/docs/tvsports.pdf

NWHL. (n.d.). *National Women's Hockey League.* Retrieved from http://www.nwhl.ca/

Pietrusza, D. (1998). *Judge and jury: The life and times of Judge Kenesaw Mountain Landis.* Philadelphia, PA: Taylor Trade Publishing.

Peterson, A. M. (2014, August 24). Women's World Cup turf war heats up. *Yahoo! News.* Retrieved from http://news.yahoo.com/womens-world-cup-turf-war-heats-073726618--spt.html

Riebock, A. (2012). *Sexualized representation of female athletes in the media: How does it affect collegiate female athlete body perceptions?* (Master's thesis, Texas Tech University, Lubbock, Texas). Retrieved from http://repositories.tdl.org/ttu-ir/handle/2346/45298

Russian official not sorry for referring to Serena, Venus as "Williams brothers." (2014, October 21). *New York Post.* Retrieved from http://nypost.com/2014/10/21/russian-official-not-sorry-for-calling-serena-venus-williams-brothers/

Schmalz, D. L., & Kerstetter, D. L. (2006). Girlie girls and manly men: Children's stigma consciousness of gender in sports and physical activities. *Journal of Leisure Research, 38*(4), 536-557.

Sousa, P., Rebelo, A., & Brito, J. (2013). Injuries in amateur soccer players on artificial turf: A one-season prospective study. *Physical Therapy in Sport, 14*(3), 146-151. doi:10.1016/j.ptsp.2012.05.003

Sullivan, J. (2014, June 21). Soccer superstar Hope Solo jailed, accused of domestic violence. *The Seattle Times.* Retrieved from http://www.seattletimes.com/seattle-news/soccer-superstar-hope-solo-jailed-accused-of-domestic-violence/

Trujillo, N. (1991). Hegemonic masculinity on the mound: Media representations of Nolan Ryan and American sports culture. *Critical Studies in Media Communication, 8*(3), 290-308. doi:10.1080/15295039109366799

Wang, S. (2006). Sports complex: The science behind fanatic behavior. *Observer, 19*(5).

USA Hockey. (n.d.) *Women's hockey history.* Retrieved from http://olympics.usahockey.com/page/show/1105636-history-of-women-s-hockey

Yu, V. (1993). Portrayals of females in sport picture books. *Melpomene Journal, 12*, 14-16.

An Interview with Erik Mebust

Hometown: *Cooperstown, NY*

Major: *English*

Hobbies: *Swimming, writing.*

Do/did you like Geneseo? Why did you choose to come to Geneseo?

Erik: I chose Geneseo for the value. For someone who wanted to study English Literature, racking up $200,000 of debt did not make very much sense. I also really liked several of Geneseo's institutions, like the Edgar Fellows program and the fact that everyone has to take two semesters of Humanities.

I do like Geneseo. I have had a good, though imperfect, experience here and it has given me incredible opportunities that made me grow personally and intellectually.

Why do you feel that GREAT Day is important?

A lot of important and interesting campus pursuits would go completely unnoticed if not for this opportunity to display them in a concentrated form.

How did it feel to present your work at GREAT Day?

It felt validating. We work hard, why should we not celebrate it?

Words and Icons in Crashaw's "The Flaming Heart"

Erik Mebust

Richard Crashaw represents an interesting intersection of several social and literary forces at work during his time. Crashaw was born in 1613; he began his life as the son of a Puritan and ended it as a Catholic priest (Greenblatt, 2012, pp. 1740-1741). He was educated in Cambridge, then served as an Anglican priest, published his poetry, carved wood, composed music, and painted. In 1644, Crashaw fled from Cromwell's advance to the mainland of Europe, where he converted entirely to Catholicism and obtained a post in Rome (Greenblatt, 2012, p. 1741). Crashaw's work lends itself well to a variety of labels, especially as part of the metaphysical literary movement and the continental baroque movement. With the central role religion played in his life, it is not surprising that Crashaw's most important and lasting works are the emblem poems and devotional lyrics published in *Steps to the Temple, The Delights of the Muses,* and *Carmen Deo Nostro.* These works made use of both imagery and words to drive home their religious meanings; the "multimedia" approach used by Crashaw represents the competing forces of iconoclast Protestantism and iconodule Catholicism at work during the age in which he lived as well as within his own mind and heart.

"The Flaming Heart," Crashaw's indictment of an unknown artist for his jejune portrayal of St. Teresa of Avila, is exemplary of emblem lyrics. In true metaphysical spirit, Crashaw (2012) rails against the unknown artist for portraying Teresa as passive and feminine, accusing the artist of misunderstanding Teresa's book and message. Even though the artist's representation is faithful to a vision described by Teresa, Crashaw (2012) contends that the image is misleading. According to Crashaw (2012), a better reading of the book would paint the image of Teresa as a dominant figure; the weapon, which pierces the hearts of those around her with a dart, would become representative of her message. Sexual imagery runs rampant in Crashaw's (2012) "The Flaming Heart";

there are descriptions of Teresa's readers as "well-pierced hearts" (p. 1754), death as "that final kiss" (p. 1755), a juxtaposition of the words "wounds and darts" (p. 1754), and the final word of the poem—"die!" (p. 1755)—would have brought to the minds of Crashaw's audience the idea of *lapetite morte.* Crashaw's poem is in accentual rhymed couplets; it employs tetrameter often, but not exclusively. The ornamental style used by Crashaw is true to his baroque influence and directly preoccupies itself with objects, an element of the style that seems to be in the spirit of Crashaw's favored religion, Catholicism. However, contradictory to what the surface interpretation of Crashaw's chosen style might suggest, deeper analysis shows that Crashaw is using the ornamental style to critique the use of objects to impart spiritual truth.

Crashaw's use of imagery is central to the poem. In fact, "The Flaming Heart" can be understood to have derived from a number of emblem poems (which featured a visual image, a Latin motto, and a poem illuminating the figurative meaning of the image) that were popular at the time. The specific image Crashaw refers to is unknown, but from his text it becomes clear that the image portrayed Teresa of Avila as a passive figure that received heaven's dart from a (dominant) seraphim. The entire poem dedicates itself to a discussion of the unknown image, an image that, as described by Matthew Horn (2008), acts as a unifying force for the verse. Horn (2008) states, "the pictorial device in the poem serves as a locus to which the subsequent verses could constantly refer" (p. 422). Horn's statement is reinforced by the constant return to different aspects of the same image within Crashaw's (2012) "The Flaming Heart," specifically in the following lines: "...whate'er this youth of fire wears fair, rosy fingers, radiant hair, glowing cheeks and glistering wings, all those fair and flagrant things..." (p. 1754). Crashaw also tells his audience how the image should be interpreted as a way of keeping tradition with the emblem poems. He says, "you must transpose the picture quite and spell it wrong to read it right" (Crashaw, 2012, p. 1753). The secret to the effectiveness of emblem poems like "The Flaming Heart" is that these poems give their readers something concrete and simple to visualize, a strategy that helps keep readers focused and engaged while the author lays out the spiritual truth.

In one sense, Crashaw's "Flaming Heart" can be labeled an anti-emblem poem because while Crashaw utilizes the benefits of imagery, he also denounces the power of images to relay religious truth. He claims that to understand the image properly, viewers must "transpose the picture quite and spell it wrong to read it right" (Crashaw, 2012, p. 1753). A few lines later, Crashaw (2012) asserts that reading Teresa's book could have brought the painter to a better understanding of her: "had thy pale-faced purple took fire from the burning cheeks of that bright book, thou wouldst on her have heaped up all that could be found seraphical" (p. 1753). He proceeds to explain how the truth is an inversion of what the painter portrayed, and in doing so, Crashaw (2012) is suggesting that words *do* have the power to impart religious truth: "In love's field was never found a nobler weapon than a wound. Love's passives are his activest part, the wounded is the wounding heart" (p. 1754). The argument presented by the quote above claims images cannot communicate seemingly contradictory aspects of the divine—but words can. However, it turns out that even words have their limitations, and Crashaw (2012) ultimately laments the fact that neither Teresa's words nor his own poetry have brought him to a union with God: "leave nothing of myself in me! Let me so read thy life that I unto all life of mine may die!" (p. 1755). This declaration can be read as an acknowledgement that even though words are superior, they are only a representation of the divine, and therefore can never replace actual divinity.

The conflict between words and images, and over which influenced audiences more effectively, was a reflection of the religious conflicts taking place during Crashaw's time. To Catholics, "books were esteemed less potent than images to impress the mind with divine truth" (Horn, 2008, p.414). Catholics supported visual pleasures that ranged from the architecture of their cathedrals (which drew the mind and the eye upwards), to the biblical paintings and mosaics that lined the walls of their churches and shrines, to pictures inscribed in Bibles in their day-to-day lives (Horn, 2008, p. 415). It was partially because of the Catholics' heavy use of icons that the Protestants rebelled. Martin Luther asserted the inability of anything besides the word of God to impart spiritual truth in his doctrine of *sola scriptura,* "through Scripture alone" (Horn, 2008, p. 415).

To acknowledge the spiritual truth through anything else besides scripture was considered idolatry by Protestants. Luther's revolt against the Catholic Church took place in the early sixteenth century, and its effects were still being felt a century later. Crashaw fled England precisely because of the advance of Cromwell's Puritan army:

> as Puritan armies moved through the country... they also undertook a crusade to stamp out idolatry in English churches, smashing religious images and stained-glass windows and lopping off the heads of statues as an earlier generation had done at the time of the English Reformation. (Greenblatt, 2012, p. 1362)

"The Flaming Heart" is expressive of Crashaw's struggle with being caught between two extremes. He had likely already converted to Catholicism, or was at least seriously considering it when he wrote the poem, as it was published after his death. One would assume that because of his close association with Catholicism, Crashaw would have been inclined to favor images but clearly he does not. Instead, in the poem, he seems to be paying homage to his Protestant roots by arguing for the supremacy of words over images. At the same time, Crashaw builds his poem entirely around an image, and the image of a Catholic doctor at that. Clearly Crashaw approached his religion partly with intellect, and was bereaved with questions of faith that neither side could totally satisfy.

Crashaw's method indicates a faith in reason that might further illuminate his preference of words. He can be categorized as one of the metaphysical poets, whose work was characterized by speculation and by abstract conceits such as the replacement image of Teresa. Crashaw (2012) offers: "give him the veil, give her the dart" (p. 1754). The new image represents a more sophisticated understanding of Teresa, and like other metaphysical conceits, to be understood, it requires abstract thought and careful consideration. This "concern with the role of reason in faith" characterizes Crashaw's personal practice of religion (Russell, 2009, p. 120). It is most likely for this reason that he takes words as the herald of divine truth; while images were used to instruct common people about the important stories and doctrines of Catholicism, it is only through words that the great minds of Christianity have been able to question and puzzle over the mysteries of God. Great triumphs of doctrine were not made with images of biblical scenes or churches—they were made through debates and arguments from many men and women over many years. Crashaw *proves* that words are superior to images. After he shows how flawed the artist's conception is, he uses words to re-interpret the image in a way that displays understanding of the power Teresa gained from being pierced by the seraphim:

> But if it be the frequent fate of worst faults to be fortunate; if all's prescription and proud wrong hearkens not to an humble song… Leave her alone the Flaming Heart. Leave her that, and thou shalt leave her not one loose shaft but love's whole quiver. (Crashaw, 2012, p. 1754)

Yet Crashaw also acknowledges the hard truth: all of the doctrinal advancement made in more than a thousand years has not brought anyone to a perfect understanding of God, and it has brought very few into a union with Him. While he derides the artist for his poor understanding of Teresa, Crashaw must also concede that the higher level of understanding Teresa's words have imparted to him has not delivered him to a union with God.

Crashaw struggles with questions that deal with achieving a union with God. By inclination he favors an intellectual approach, trying to apprehend God by understanding His mysteries. For this reason, he favors words over icons as a means to accessing divinity, which represents a reversal of his progress from Protestantism to Catholicism, even though he was in the process of converting or actually practicing Catholicism as a priest when he wrote it. He disparages others such as the artist in "The Flaming Heart" for not understanding holy mysteries at the level he does, while admitting that his higher level of intellectual understanding has not brought him to union with God either. However, Crashaw does not despair, and the reader is left with a sense that while it is impossible to truly capture the nature of God in words or images, "[striving and failing to] to sing the name which none can say sings succeeds in summoning the object of that name and earning His love" (Russell, 2009, p. 144).

REFERENCES

Crashaw, R. (2012). The flaming heart. In S. Greenblatt (Ed.), *Norton Anthology of English Literature* (9th ed., Vol. 1, 1753-1755). New York, NY: W. W. Norton & Company.

Greenblatt, S. (Ed.). (2012). Richard Crashaw ca. 1613-1649. In *Norton Anthology of English Literature* (9th ed., Vol. 1, pp. 1740-1741). New York, NY: W. W. Norton & Company.

Horn, M. (2008). A safe space for the texted icon: Richard Crashaw's use of the emblem tradition in his devotional lyrics. *Exemplaria, 20*(4), 410-429. doi:10.1179/175330708X371438

Russell, W. (2009). "Spell it wrong to read it right": Crashaw's assessment of human language. *John Donne Journal: Studies in the Age of Donne, 28*, 119-145.

An Interview with Songyi Paik

Hometown: *Daejeon, South Korea*

Major: *Economics*

Hobbies: *Listening to music and radio, swimming, traveling, drawing beautiful calligraphy.*

Do/did you like Geneseo? Why did you choose to come to Geneseo?

Songyi: I chose Geneseo because there was less burden of tuition fees and because it was a liberal arts college (meaning I could immerse myself in other subjects necessary for deep learning).

I do like Geneseo. I've learned about the benefits of a small town and campus. When I first arrived at Geneseo, everyone was very nice and kind. Since it was my first time in America, it was a great environment to be in while I was adapting to American culture. Because there aren't many graduate school students at Geneseo, I am able to talk with my professor more easily and frequently. It is good to learn from professors and not only TAs.

Why do you feel that GREAT Day is important?

GREAT Day is a time to present what I learned and found in and out of class. While I prepared the GREAT Day presentation, I met with my professor many times and learned how to apply what I learned in class to my research. Learning and practicing are different in some sense. Practicing allows me to understand and remember more principles and theories. Also, getting feedback for presentation helps me further develop my thoughts and research paper.

How did it feel to present your work at GREAT Day?

I was very nervous to present in front of people. Usually I presented in class and it was less nerve-wracking because people in class were my friends and had the same major. So, I had to prepare my presentation for people from other majors to understand my work. It is one of the first steps preparing for graduate school. I learned the format of a PowerPoint in the academic field from my professor. In graduate school I will be posed hard or unexpected questions. During GREAT Day, I learned how to how to respond to difficult questions. For example, if I really do not know a concept, I accept that I do not know and I also prepare additional slides to explain other things which I studied but did not present because of the short time alloted for my presentation.

The U.S. Consumption Analysis: Using a Linear Regression Model

Songyi Paik

ABSTRACT

Recent U.S. consumption has decreased, although it is the most significant factor in economic growth. Using a linear regression model, this paper shows that consumption is influenced by disposable income, oil price, and recession, but is not influenced by interest rates. It will also discuss policies regarding how to improve consumption. The result that the interest rate does not influence consumption is consistent with the view of John Maynard Keynes, but the Granger Causality test implies that past interest rates might be possible to change current consumption considering time lag.

INTRODUCTION

During the Great Recession, which lasted from 2008 to 2009, the deterioration of consumer expenditures lasted longer than in any of the other recessions since the 1970s. This consumption trend assumes the economy needs a great deal of time to fully recover (Petev & Pistaferz, 2012). Figure 1 shows there was a steep downward trend in consumption during financial crisis, and in 60 years the overall spending trend (blue line) has declined. Considering that consumption is a key factor to economic growth in the U.S., the decreasing consumption trend can possibly have a negative impact on economic growth. Consumer spending accounts for about 70% percent of economic activity in the U.S. The Marginal Propensity to Consume (MPC), which is the proportion of additional income that is spent on consumption, is around 0.7 while the European MPC is around 0.2 (Carroll, Slacalek, & Tokuoka, 2014). Compared to other countries, the U.S. consumer expenditure has a considerable portion of earnings and offers increased economic development. Therefore, the government has to promote increased spending. This paper will show factors which influ-

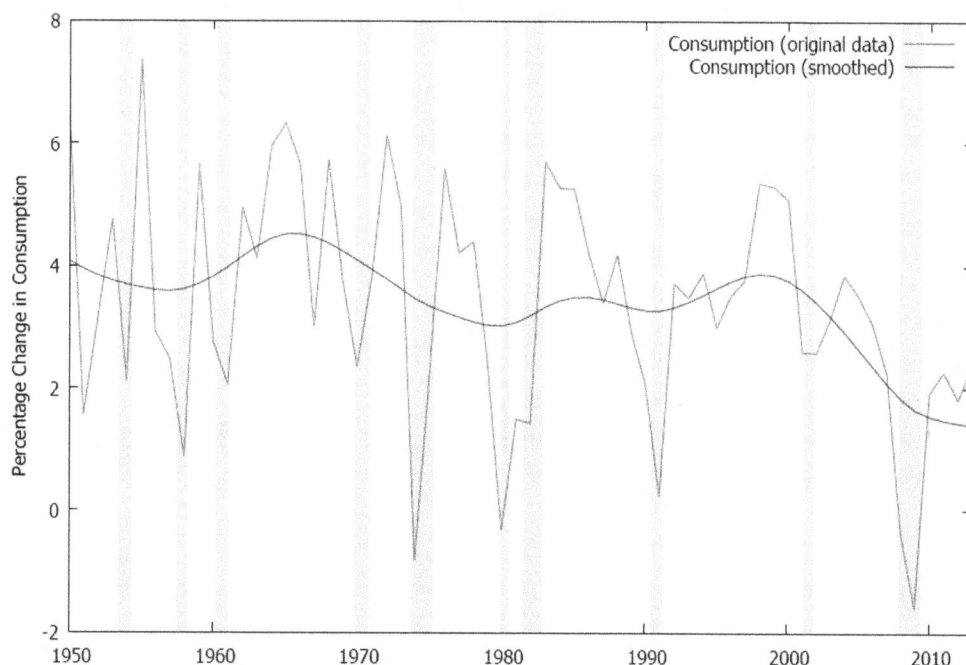

Figure 1. Decomposing Consumption Series (shade: NBER recessions)

ence consumption using a linear regression model, and based on these components, it will suggest policies the government should conduct to encourage spending.

Measuring Influential Factors on Consumption

A Theoretical Model

$$ \overset{(+)}{} \quad \overset{(-)}{} \quad \overset{(-)}{} \quad \overset{(-)}{} $$

$$ (1) \quad C_t = \beta_0 + \beta_1 Yd_t + \beta_2 r_t + \beta_3 Oil_t + \beta_2 R_1 + e_t $$

The dependent variable measured for this paper is the consumption in unit of percentage change. As John Maynard Keynes (1973) first mentioned in the consumption function, disposable income is one of the most important factors as an independent variable. When disposable income increases, people can afford to consume more, expecting a positive sign of the coefficient. To avoid a non-stationary time series problem and interpret the implication of the coefficient properly, the unit is the percent change of disposable income. This paper assumes that the interest rate (r) can affect the dependent variable with negative correlation. This is because when the interest rate increases, people can save more to get higher interest; when the mortgage rate is low, people will be more apt to buy houses because of the low interest rate. The oil price has a dollar unit per barrel and is predicted to have a negative sign because Mehra and Petersen (2005) stated that oil price increases have a negative effect on spending. Moreover, recently declining crude oil prices from the fourth quarter of 2014 have also influenced consumption. Eric Morath (2014) argues "Spending is being boosted by falling oil prices." In this sense, it is worthwhile to include crude oil price as an independent variable to apply and observe the recent trends of oil prices. In recession periods, people tend to spend less to protect themselves against the danger of economic risk and postpone purchases after recessions. If a year had a recession period of over six months, this year is assigned a 1 as a dummy variable.

Estimating Regression Line

$$ \overset{(+)}{} \quad \overset{(-)}{} \quad \overset{(-)}{} \quad \overset{(-)}{} $$

$$ (2) \quad C_t = 2.4 + 0.67 Yd_t + 0.03 r_t - 0.01 Oil_t - 1.24 R_1 $$

Each coefficient's interpretation is the following: The 1% increase in disposable income raises consumption by 0.67%, and the 1% point increase in interest rates brings a 0.03% increase in consumption. When the crude oil price increases by one dollar, people spend less by 0.01%. In the recession period, consumer spending decreased by 1.24%.

Sensitivity Analysis

To check the fit of the estimated equation and degree of reliability, this paper conducted several sensitivity analyses with the results in Table 1. An asterisk in the p-value row indicates how the coefficient is significant. As the table shows, the interest rate is not statistically significant and has an unexpected positive sign.

Except for the coefficient of interest rates, the other coefficients are statistically significant: disposable income and recession are at the 1% level and oil price is at the 5% level. In macroeconomics, the components of GDP or total income are given by Equation 3. This insignificant relationship between interest rate and consumption confirms that the interest rate (r) has a large impact on investment, (I), not consumption, (C), as income Equation 3 indicates in macroeconomics.

$$ (3) \quad Y = C(Y-T) + I(r) + G + NX(\Xi) $$

The adjusted R-squared is 0.72 and the p-value of the F test is almost zero, which can reject the null

Table 1					
Summary Statistics : Annual Time Series 1950-2013					
	Const	Yd_t	r_t	Oil_t	R_1
coefficient	2.4	0.67	0.03	-0.01	-1.24
std. error	0.36	0.09	0.05	0.005	0.37
t-ratio	6.60	7.84	0.72	-2.01	-3.38
p-value	1.30e-08***	9.95e-011***	0.4773	0.0489**	0.0013***
VIF	--	1.402	1.132	1.251	1.24

F(3, 60)	37.76	P-value(F)	1.20e-15
R-squared	0.72	**R**-squared	0.70
Durbin-Watson	2.35	White's test for heteroskedasticity	p-value = 0.95

Source: Author calculations.
*** Significant at the 1 percent level.
** Significant at the 5 percent level.

hypothesis that all coefficients are equal to zero. Both results mean that the overall fit is good. The Durbin-Watson test for detecting serial correlation shows 2.35. It is greater than the upper critical value of the 1% one sided test (1.57), which cannot reject the null hypothesis of no positive serial correlation. The p-value of White's test for heteroskedasticity is 0.95 and we cannot reject the null hypothesis of homoscedasticity, implying that there is no heteroskedasticity. To test the existence of multicollinearity, Variance Inflation Factor (VIF) is useful as an indicator of the test. The values of VIF of all coefficients are around 1, which means there is no multicollinearity. These sensitivity analyses demonstrate that this equation is reliable overall.

POLICIES TO PROMOTE CONSUMPTION

Considering the decreasing trend of consumption and that consumer spending is a key driver of economic growth, the government must encourage public consumption. In order to increase demand of goods and services, the government can decrease oil prices by increasing oil production. However, the crude oil price is influenced by international oil production as well. Also, the value of the Oil coefficient is so small that this paper will focus on disposable income policies.

Disposable income is a big portion of consumption change, and therefore raising income is a substantially effective way to increase consumption and further economic growth. The policies can be implemented through different means in both the short and long run. In the short run, the government can decrease the income tax. As Equation 3 indicates, the function of consumption (C) is composed of disposable income (Y-T) and it is influenced by tax (T). If the government gives tax cuts, it will lead to increased disposable income as well as consumption. In 1964, President Kennedy made substantial cuts to personal income tax and growth in real GDP raised from 5.3% to 6.0% in a year along with increased consumption (Mankiw, 2010). As President Kennedy's economic policy of tax cuts shows, reducing taxes can bring about an economic boom and a decline in the unemployment rate.

To effectively increase consumption, the government can decrease income tax, especially to low income classes because the MPC of the lower income group is bigger than that of a high income group. If lower income groups receive tax cuts, they will consume more than the high income bracket. Considering the tax multiplier in Equation 4, if the MPC is higher (low income group), the change of increase in income resulting from a $1 decrease in taxes is greater than that for a high income group. Thus, with increased income, the lower income group will spend more than the other. Therefore, more tax cuts to the low income group encourage them to promote expenditure effectively in the short run.

$$(4) \quad \frac{\Delta Y}{\Delta T} = \frac{-MPC}{1-MPC}$$

In the long run, the government has to increase employment rates because when people get jobs and earn money, they will consume. Using the data set of the original consumption (C) and an additional dataset of unemployment rates, the correlation between two variables is around -0.32, which is significant at the 1% level. It implies that policies that raise employment rates increase not only consumption, but also economic growth. To expand employment, the government can manage employment agencies more efficiently to match jobs between potential workers and employers. The agencies disseminate information about job vacancies and thus help the unemployed to find appropriate jobs quickly. In addition, the government has to give a chance for the unemployed to participate in retraining programs. This can also relieve problems from sectoral shifts, changes in demand among industries and regions. Both employment agencies and retraining programs help to decrease frictional unemployment, which occurs during the job search process.

CONCLUSION

This paper has shown key factors of aggregate consumption such as disposable income, crude oil prices, and recession, but not the interest rate in accordance with the macroeconomic model of GDP, Equation 3. The estimated regression model documented that the coefficient of disposable income takes a big share of influence on consumption among other independent variables, and practical policies were mentioned to increase disposable income.

Although the data set and estimated equation indicate that interest rates do not influence consumption, there is still a question about this result as the correlation between interest rates and consumption can possibly exist: if the interest rate is high, will people save more and consume less to receive interest, or if mortgage rates are low, will people buy houses due to reducing the burden of paying higher interest rates? To confirm the correlation between interest rates and consumption, this paper conducts the Granger Causality test, which shows bilateral ways of interaction between two variables considering time lag.

(5) $r_t = \beta_0 + \beta_1 C_{t-1} + \ldots + \beta_4 C_{t-4} + \beta_5 r_{t-1} + \ldots + \beta_8 r_{t-4} + \varepsilon_t$

All lags of Consumption $F_{(4, 51)} = 0.39399\ [0.8120]$

(6) $C_t = \beta_0 + \beta_1 r_{t-1} + \ldots + \beta_4 r_{t-4} + \beta_5 C_{t-1} + \ldots + \beta_8 C_{t-4} + \varepsilon_t$

All lags of Consumption $F_{(4, 51)} = 0.39399\ [0.8120]$

The p-value (0.8120) of the F test from Equation 5 means that consumption does not Granger cause interest rates because it cannot reject the null hypothesis that all lagged coefficients of C are equal to zero. However, the p-value (0.0140) of Equation 6 shows that interest rates do Granger cause consumption. This result implies that past interest rates might be able to change current consumption. If we analyze this relation in different ways (for example, dividing the time period of several years' duration or choosing other interest rates as indicators instead of 3-month treasury bills) there may be a different result. In this sense, it is worth analyzing the relation between interest rates and consumption in future research.

Appendix

Running a Regression Without Interest Rate Variable

The interest rate can be an irrelevant variable in the original model because the p-value is too high. Simply removing the irrelevant variable is not an appropriate treatment, but this paper will show how the result changes and try what could be done.

In Table 2, the levels of all coefficients decrease slightly compared with Table 1. Adjusted R-squared increases marginally, and the values of Durbin-Watson and VIF of each variable decrease slightly as well.

Generally, there is no big difference in statistical significance in the models between including and excluding the interest rate.

Table 2				
Summary Statistics Without Interest Rate Variable: Annual Time Series 1950-2013				
	Const	Yd_t	Oil_t	R_t
coefficient	2.47	0.69	-0.01	-1.17
std. error	0.35	0.83	0.005	0.35
t-ratio	7.16	8.25	-1.91	-3.32
p-value	1.36e-09***	1.87e-011***	0.0608*	0.0015***
VIF	--	1.332	1.196	1.161

$F_{(3, 60)}$	50.58468	P-value(F)	1.98e-16
R-squared	0.716652	**R**-squared	0.702485
Durbin-Watson	2.30	White's test for heteroskedasticity	p-value = 0.98

Source: Author calculations.
*** Significant at the 1 percent level.
* Significant at the 10 percent level.

Running a Regression Without Recession Variable

The recession and consumption variable might affect each other because the change in consumption is influenced by recession at first, but over time, decreased consumer spending can deepen recession. By eliminating the recession variable, this paper will observe how outcome will change.

Table 3				
Summary Statistics Without Interest Rate Variable: Annual Time Series 1950-2013				
	Const	Yd_t	r_t	R_t
coefficient	2.12	0.78	-0.01	-0.01
std. error	0.38	0.09	0.05	0.01
t-ratio	5.53	8.99	-0.17	-1.84
p-value	7.45e-07***	1.02e-012***	0.8636	0.0703*
VIF	--	1.217	1.052	1.251

$F_{(3, 60)}$	39.66354	P-value(F)	2.96e-14
R-squared	0.664787	**R**-squared	0.648026
Durbin-Watson	2.01	White's test for heteroskedasticity	p-value = 0.55

Source: Author calculations.
*** Significant at the 1 percent level.
* Significant at the 10 percent level.

Compared to Table 1, the statistical analyses excluding recession show that the p-values of the coefficient of interest rates and Oil increase, which further reduces statistical significance. Adjusted R-squared decreases by 0.05 and the values of VIF of disposable income and interest rate coefficients decrease in small amounts. The interest rate is still statistically insignificant and the overall fit of a regression decreases.

DATA SOURCES

Consumption: Percent change of real personal consumption expenditures (Sources: Federal Reserve Bank of St. Louis' *Real Personal Consumption Expenditures.*)

Disposable Income: Percent change of real disposable personal income (Sources: Federal Reserve Bank of St. Louis' *Real disposable personal income: Per capita.*)

Interest Rate: Percent of 3-month treasury bill (Sources: Federal Reserve Bank of St. Louis' *3-Month Treasury Bill: Secondary Market Rate.*)

Oil: Real crude oil in US dollars per barrel (Sources: ChartsBin's *Historical Crude Oil prices, 1861 to Present.*)

Recession: A dummy variable equal to 1 if recession, 0 otherwise (Sources: National Bureau of Economic Research's *US Business Cycle Expansions and Contractions.*)

Unemployment Rate: Percent of unemployment rate (Sources: Federal Reserve Bank of St. Louis' *Civilian Unemployment Rate.*)

REFERENCES

Carroll, C. D., Slacalek, J., & Tokuoka, K. (2014). The distribution of wealth and MPC: Implications of new European data. *The American Economic Review, 104*(5), 107-111. doi:10.1257/aer.104.5.107

Keynes, J. M. (1973). *The general theory of employment, interest, and money.* London, England: Macmillan.

Mankiw, N. G. (2010). *Macroeconomics* (7th ed.). New York, NY: Worth Publishers.

Mehra, Y. P. & Peterson, J. D. (2005). Oil prices and consumer spending. *Federal Reserve Bank of Richmond Economic Quarterly, 91*(3), 53-72.

Morath, E. (2014, December 23). U.S. consumer spending accelerates in November. *Wall Street Journal.* Retrieved from http://on.wsj.com/1xdCW4k

Petev, I. D. & Pistaferz, L. (2012). *Consumption in the Great Recession.* Stanford, CA: Stanford Center on Poverty and Inequality.

An Interview with Nicole Theal

Hometown: *Buffalo, NY*

Major: *International Relations and French*

Hobbies: *Swimming and knitting.*

Do/did you like Geneseo? Why did you choose to come to Geneseo?

Nicole: I loved Geneseo—enough to convince my younger brother to attend Geneseo as well! I attended Geneseo because it was an affordable, close-to-home college that was committed to liberal arts. The fact that the campus was beautiful, with ivy covered buildings and a picturesque gazebo also helped sway my decision.

Why do you feel that GREAT Day is important?

GREAT Day is extremely important, and not only as a line on a resume and a talking point at interviews. It helps individuals gain confidence in their research and their presentation skills.

How did it feel to present your work at GREAT Day?

I was extremely proud to have presented at GREAT Day two years in a row. I was also happy that my family and academic advisors were able to come and support me each year.

Legislative Rape Reforms: Issues in India and the U.S.

Nicole Theal

On December 12, 2012, an Indian physiotherapy student was the victim of a vicious gang rape. While the student succumbed to her injuries, the incident was successful in prompting unprecedented dialogue about sexual violence against women. This dialogue primarily condemned India, a country which is deemed the rape capital of the world (Bhowmick, 2013). However, according to official statistics, the number of rapes in the United States is 13 times higher than the number of reported rapes in India (Bialik, 2013). This is especially shocking considering the huge difference in population size between the two countries. The U.S. falls behind India's estimated population of 1.23 billion and reaches an estimated sum of 318 million inhabitants (Central Intelligence Agency [CIA], 2015a; CIA, 2015b). Upon recognizing the need for change, both governments enacted legislative reforms to lessen the increasing rate of sexual violence. Nonetheless, these legislative reforms have been unsuccessful in their prevention of rape due to the weak and patriarchal institutions charged with enforcing them.

As a group, women face major obstacles in their attempts at gaining social equality. Globally, only 22% of all parliamentary positions are held by women (Inter-Parliamentary Union [IPU], 2015). On average, women receive less pay than their male counterparts for equal work (Department of Economic and Social Affairs, 2010). In addition, one in three women have experienced some form of sexual violence within their lifetime (London School of Hygiene and Tropical Medicine, 2013). This violence is particularly abhorrent, considering the severe and damaging physical, emotional, social, and economic impacts. Physical consequences experienced by the victims generally include pain, bruising, bleeding, and broken limbs. Common and troublesome mental health symptoms after an assault include depression, PTSD, alcohol or drug dependence, and anxiety. In addition, many estimates indicate that sexual assault victims are four times more likely to consider suicide (Koss, 1993).

Socially, rape victims are often ostracized by their communities and families due to the shame and stigma associated with extramarital intercourse (McGlynn & Munro, 2010). Victims are sometimes viewed as tainted and dishonored, and in India, this renders many unable to marry. After an assault, victims also incur high financial costs due to medical treatments and lost paid hours. In fact, a study conducted by the Center for Disease Control in 2003 reported that the average treatments for victims cost about $2,084 (The White House Council on Women and Girls & the Office of the Vice President, 2014). On a macroeconomic scale, figures estimate that every rape costs the U.S. economy around $87,000. This figure considers the costs of medical expenses, the victim's lost productivity, the cost of law enforcement and an intangible decrease in the victim's quality of life (The White House Council on Women and Girls & the Office of the Vice President, 2014).

Due to the grave consequences of sexual attacks and the high rates of violent sexual occurrences in societies around the world, women live in near constant fear of such attacks. Consequently, Catharine MacKinnon described rape as "'an act of dominance over women that works systematically to maintain a gender-stratified society in which women occupy a disadvantaged status as the appropriate victims and targets of sexual aggression'" (as cited in Annavarapu, 2013, p. 253). Motivations for rape are primarily rooted in power dynamics, as opposed to sexual urges. Jessica Valenti (2014), a prominent feminist writer, introduced the concept of a "rape schedule" (pp. 66-67), describing the changes women undertake in order to reduce their risk of rape. According to Valenti (2014), these changes are often small and unconscious, consistent of actions such as avoiding certain streets at night, or walking home with keys

93

between knuckles. However, these small changes represent significant insecurity, whereby women can never truly feel safe from harm (Valenti, 2014).

Specific causes of rape vary across societies. Firstly, gender norms and roles largely impact rape and sexual assault rates. Rape and sexual assault occur more frequently in societies where gender roles and behaviors are clearly delineated and limited (Shaw & Lee, 2008). Additionally, sexual violence against women occurs more frequently in societies where masculinity is valued over femininity, which is true concerning most societies. When this leverage of masculinity occurs, young boys are often taught to suppress their emotions and to conflate their sexual potency with power. Comparatively, young girls are taught to be weak and dependent on the men in their lives (Shaw & Lee, 2008).

Boys are traditionally introduced to their male privilege at an early age. Consequently, many men start to internalize an entitled mentality, leading to what scholars often refer to as the rape spectrum. This describes the range of behaviors men often engage in due to their unchecked belief of superiority over women, which in extreme cases can lead to rape (Shaw & Lee, 2008). Furthermore, this privileged attitude can lead to a cultural backlash against women's freedoms and rights. This backlash is often associated with violence; when men feel vulnerable, they use violence to forcibly regain their power. Lastly, the eroticization and eventual normalization of sexual violence is another key factor leading to high rates of rape and sexual assault (Shaw & Lee, 2008). This process can occur through advertisements, films, and popular songs. However, the main culprit in eroticizing sexual violence is the pornography industry (Shaw & Lee, 2008).

Many of these conditions exist in both India and the U.S., where, despite common perceptions, women have yet to achieve full gender equality. Women in the U.S. experience discrimination in numerous aspects of society. Research conducted by the National Science Foundation (2013) on this subject demonstrates that women are less likely to pursue a degree or career in the STEM fields; over 12.52 million men currently work as scientists and engineers, compared to 10.69 million women. Relatively, women do not earn the same amount of money as men in the work-

force. One of the reasons behind this inequality is that women disproportionately work lower-paying jobs and careers. Thus, women are more likely than men to live in poverty.

Narrowly defined gender roles within the U.S. elucidate the persistent problem of sexual violence against women. Mainstream pop culture projects an acceptable range of gender specific traits and behaviors unto men and women. Men are praised for their strength, power, and independence and condemned for signs of weakness. Women, on the other hand, are encouraged to be weak, beautiful, and sexually submissive to male advances (Shaw & Lee, 2008). These stereotypes are prevalent in current songs, advertisements and, most importantly, films. Many studies have attempted to quantify the specific ways that male representation differs from female representation in films. Recent studies by the Geena Davis Institute on gender in the media conclude that women in films are underrepresented in the workforce, are more likely to be thin, beautiful, and sexualized, and are less likely to have specific career ambitions compared to their male counterparts (Smith & Cook 2008).

Correlatively, the U.S. experienced much cultural backlash as a result of the increasing equality and freedoms of women during the second half of the twentieth century. Due to the large number of men overseas serving in the army during World War II there was an increased need for women in the labor force. As a result, Deckard's research shows that by the end of the 1960s, more than 50% of American women worked outside the home (as cited in Odem & Clay-Warner, 1998, p. 40). When the men returned from war, many of them viewed this change as "an attack on traditional roles and a defiance of chivalry" (Odem & Clay-Warner, 1998, p. 40). Returning soldiers perceived their power structure as threatened and this caused some men to rely on physical attacks as a way of regaining superiority. In addition, social stigma was used to illegitimatize women's gained positions in the public sphere. As a result, women who exhibited newfound assertiveness and confidence in the public sphere were labelled as "loose women," who were responsible for their rapes (Odem & Clay-Warner, 1998, p. 40).

A study conducted by Cooper, Scherer, Boies, and Gordon found that over 90% of participants had accessed some form of sexually-explicit content online (as cited in Popovic, 2011, p. 450). This is an especially alarming statistic, due to recent figures estimating that over 88% of popular pornographic scenes include violent or aggressive acts (Bridges, Wosnitzer, Scharrer, Sun, & Liberman, 2010). Consequently, young boys who view this pornography begin to internalize and accept violent intercourse as normal. Many studies support this notion; their evidence reports that teenagers are frequently viewing porn as a way to gain insight on real-life sexual relations (Popovic, 2011).

Women in India have experienced a similar history of discrimination compared to the US. During the World Economic Forum in 2011, India was ranked 114 out of 134 countries in terms of gender equality (Kolaskar & Dash, 2012). This ranking reflected numerous forms of discrimination, including domestic violence, low political representation, and limited educational opportunities. According to the International Center for Research on Women, 52% of Indian women have experienced some form of sexual violence during their lifetime (Gaynair, 2011). In terms of political representation, women hold only 11% of the available political positions (IPU, 2015). Additionally, young girls are less likely to receive an education compared to their male counterparts, causing a significant gap between male and female literacy (Lama, 2014).

Female discriminations in India begins even before birth through female feticide. This is due to male children being valued for their potential monetary and social worth. Additionally, due to the deeply entrenched dowry tradition, females are viewed as future monetary burdens (Sharma, Pardasani, & Nandram, 2014). The heavy and often insurmountable burden of dowry could be understood through the recent incident that took place in December, 2014, when a woman was found drowned along with her two young girls. Authorities released a statement indicating that the woman drowned the two girls and then committed suicide, due to her husband's persistent and violent demands for more dowry payments ("Fed Up With Additional Dowry Demands," 2014). Consequently, the population of India is skewed, with 940 female babies born for every 1,000 males (Sharma et al., 2014).

Discrimination also manifests itself in specific gender roles in Indian culture. Recent studies have shown that women in India are still relegated to the private sphere, where they are dependent on the males in their lives, responsible for cooking, cleaning and child rearing (Gaynair, 2011). In a recent study organized by the International Center for Research on Women, only around 16% of the Indian men surveyed responded that they participated in domestic chores (Gaynair, 2011). As a result of this low percentage, Indian boys are taught by example that women are subservient, dependent, and should remain at home. Additionally, many Indian women have come to accept subservience, viewing it as a normal and acceptable position in society. A recent UNICEF (2014) report stated that over 50% of the young Indian girls surveyed believed that wife beating was justified in certain circumstances such as leaving the house without male permission, refusing sex, or burning food.

However, due to progressive economic reforms in the 1990s, opportunities for women outside the home have drastically increased in India. Since these economic reforms have been taking place, large numbers of women are gaining education and entering the workforce. A recent study by the International Monetary Fund estimated that the 2012 female labor force participation in India was around 33% (Das, Jain-Chandra, Kochhar, & Kumar, 2015, p. 4). This amounts to a significant increase in women's participation in the public sphere. However, this increase has not been received positively by all of India. Similar to the history of the U.S., women in India's public sphere are deemed by many as morally loose and dishonorable (Odem & Clay-Warner, 1998). In the recent Delhi gang rape, one of the rapists blamed the victim for the attack; he claimed she was responsible because she was in public with a male and without familial supervision (Roberts, 2015).

Public facilities and transportation systems in India also reflect male bias in their limited provision of safe and accessible public amenities for women. In New Delhi, a recent study indicates that there are approximately 1,534 public toilets for men, compared to 132 toilets provided for women (Yardley, 2012). Many of these restrooms close at night, often around 9PM, and there is speculation that this might be a way of implicitly indicating that women should not be outside the home after this hour. This implemented curfew is nearly impossible to keep for many young women employed in the telecommunications sector (Padmaja, 2008). Due to U.S. outsourcing, many telecommunications jobs operate on the U.S. time schedule, translating to late hours in India. On a positive note, Mumbai's public transport system provides an example of a small, successful initiative that has increased women's sense of security and confidence. The transportation company designed specific train carts reserved solely for women after recognizing the increasing number of women traveling within Mumbai (Phadke, Ranade, & Khan, 2013). As a result, women feel affirmed in their freedom to travel safely and independently around the city.

One of the main contributing factors to the high rates of sexual violence against women is the caste system. The long-entrenched caste system is a hierarchal structure that delineates individuals' social functions based on heredity. The higher castes are associated with religion, purity and honor. Upper-caste women are traditionally forced to remain pure in order to prevent inter-caste relations that would undermine the power structure. However, lower-caste women, especially Dalit girls, are viewed as having no social need for purity. This rationale is used to justify the rape and forced prostitution of Dalit girls in order to preserve the honor of their higher caste counterparts (Kristof & WuDunn, 2009).

In sum, women in both India and the U.S. are at high risk of experiencing sexual violence. In order to protect their citizens from this gendered violence, the U.S and Indian governments have incorporated detailed provisions for rape victims and punishments for perpetrators into legislation and regulations. However, the two government systems use significantly different language concerning sexual violence against women. According to the Indian Penal Code, "rape" is defined as a man engaged in intercourse with a woman either against her will, without her consent, with coerced or false consent, with a woman who is unable to understand and give consent, or with a girl under the age of 15 (S. 375, The Indian Penal Code, 1860). In comparison, the United States federal code uses the term "sexual abuse," defined as: any sexual act that is either forced, committed against one who is physically or mentally unable to give consent, or against someone's expressed desire (109A U.S.C. § 2241, 2013). However, in the U.S., the majority of

rape cases are under their respective state's jurisdiction; among the 50 states, the terms and provisions vary in terms of rape and sexual assault, but share common principles.

According to official statistics, India experiences a relatively low number of rape cases, with only two victims per 100,000 people (Bialik, 2013). This low number mirrors formal legal recognition of women's rights and equality. Since independence from Britain, India has promulgated a variety of statutes empowering and protecting women. These range from equal protection under the law in Article 14 of the Constitution of India, to positive discrimination in favor of women guaranteed in Article 15 (Yee, 2013).

However, these formal laws do not match the current lives of many Indian women, and this low rape statistic is considered largely inaccurate due to India's patriarchal society, which punishes women for reporting their rape. Underreporting occurs in every society because of the private and often humiliating nature of sexual violence (McGlynn & Munro, 2010). However, many consider underreporting to be more prevalent in India due to its highly entrenched patriarchal culture and institutions. As previously mentioned, women run the risk of being ostracized from their community if they report an assault. Additionally, many women are coerced or encouraged to marry their rapists in order to salvage their honor. Police officers are the main proponents of this practice, who assume their primary role in rape cases is to serve the interests of the victim's families (Human Rights Watch, 2009).

Before the 1970s and 1980s, the women's movement focused on increasing jobs and education for high and middle-caste women. The movement gained a broader base of support after the publication of *Towards Equality* in May, 1975 (Guha et al.). The 480-page document was the product of the UN's Committee on the Status of Women in India (Calman, 1989). It included shocking statistics demonstrating the numerous ways in which women were discriminated against in India. The topics ranged from skewed sex ratios to the limited opportunities for girl's education (Calman, 1989). Consequently, the women's movement, composed of women from different socioeconomic statuses, religions, and geographic areas, shifted its focus to reforming India's outdated rape laws (Katzenstein, 1989). The rape reform movement of the 1970s and 1980s was triggered by the Mathura rape case in 1972. Mathura, an illiterate, poor, 16-year-old girl, was brutally raped by two on-duty police officers while in their custody. Mathura s had been placed in police custody by her brother after a failed attempt to elope with her boyfriend (Yee, 2013). During the resulting case, *Tukaram v. State of Maharashtra* (1979), the court found the officers innocent after considering the absence of physical evidence. Mathura's characterization as a loose, morally-repugnant girl also influenced the court's decision, which claimed that her honor had been tarnished by her illicit affair with her boyfriend (Yee, 2013). While the decision was overturned by the high court, the Supreme Court later reinstated the first court's decision, claiming that Mathura consented to the intercourse (Katzenstein, 1989, p .62). In response, four female law professors at Delhi University penned an open letter to the chief justice to criticize the ruling.

The increasing pressure from the women's movement influenced Indian government to make multiple amendments to the Indian Penal Code during the 1980s. After the reforms, the minimum mandatory punishment was increased to seven years for rape and ten years for aggravated rape, including gang rapes, custodial rapes, statutory rape, and the rape of pregnant women (Yee, 2013). Other small victories included the successful establishment of counseling centers, short-term shelters, and crime cells specifically dedicated to violence against women (Kolaskar & Dash, 2012).

Unfortunately, this seemingly successful campaign did not curb rape incidents. Since these reforms, the number of reported rapes has increased from 3,000 in the early 1970s to more than 20,000 in 2010 (Wright, 2013). According to the National Crime Records Bureau (NCRB), this statistic has continued to climb; there were more than 33,707 reported rapes in 2013 alone (Dasgupta, 2014). While this figure suggests an increased awareness which has enabled the acknowledgement of rape as well as a growth in population size, some studies suggest that the actual number of rapes might be 50 to 200 times higher (Bialik, 2013).

However, a robust and universal anti-rape campaign did not resurface in India until the brutal Delhi gang rape in 2012. On December 16, 2012, Jyoti Singh Pandey, a 23-year-old physiotherapy student, was the victim of a devastating gang rape in New Delhi, India. The victim, often referred to as "India's Daughter," was out with her male friend during the night of the attack. After watching the movie "Life of Pi," the pair boarded a private bus where they were deceived and subsequently assaulted by six men. After the male friend was physically restrained, the men took turns brutally raping Jyoti (Sharma et al., 2014). Due to the crime's incredibly violent nature, in which a metal rod was used for penetration, Jyoti was transferred to Mount Elizabeth Hospital, a top medical facility in Singapore. Thirteen days after the assault, Jyoti succumbed to her extensive, irreparable physical injuries and died ("Delhi Gang-Rape Victim Dies," 2012).

The next day, the Jawaharlal Nehru University Student's Union organized the first student protest, utilizing social media to spread awareness. Eventually, thousands of protesters occupied the streets, demanding "freedom without fear" (Drache & Velagic, 2014, p. 23). Their demands revolved around better protection and equal treatment for women, and called for institutional changes within the police, the judiciary system, and the criminal laws. In addition to the public demonstrations, the Delhi rape also gained intense media attention and scrutiny. Within two months, over 1,515 articles about the assault were published in U.S. newspapers (Drache & Velagic, 2014, p. 15).

The severe nature of the crime coupled with the intense scrutiny of the public and media caused the trial to be expedited. Consequently, within a year of the crime, four out of the six perpetrators were sentenced to death. The other two perpetrators were not tried at the same trial, one being underage (tried within the juvenile system), while the other committed suicide within his jail cell. On September 13, 2013, the four perpetrators were found guilty of attempt to murder, destruction of evidence, kidnapping or abducting, gang rape, unnatural offences, hurting in committing robbery, and common intention under the amended Indian Penal Code (Sharma et al., 2014).

The manner in which the Delhi gang rape trial proceeded is not representative of the majority of rape cases in India, however. In fact, it is argued by many that the Delhi rape was sensationalized, serving as nationalist propaganda. Jyoti, as an educated young girl from a poor family, represented the changing economic climb in India, where caste is not a binding structure. Conversely, her attackers were part of the large population of migrants seeking jobs in large cities. Their reprehensible actions were used as examples by nationalist, right-wing politicians seeking to purify India of low-caste, "backwards" migrant workers (Roychowdhury, 2013).

Quick verdicts such as the ones demonstrated in the Delhi case are extremely rare, due to the slow and overburdened nature of the Indian judicial system. A recent *Times of India* article cited that over 31 million cases are awaiting trial in the Indian judiciary system (Sinha, 2014). This backlog is especially apparent concerning rape and sexual assault cases. According to India's law minister, Ashwani Kumar, an estimated 24,000 rape cases are awaiting trial within the judicial system (Bagri, 2013). In addition, cases involving minorities, especially Dalits, are frequently overlooked or ignored. On June 28, 2012, a 15-year-old girl from a rural village was abducted by four men, tied up, and repeatedly raped. However, a year and a half later there still had been no justice on her behalf (Bagri, 2013).

In addition to the introduction of a fast track system, the Indian government commissioned a small task force and charged it with investigating the severe problem of rape in India. The task force was named the Verma Committee. Its goal was to outline potential legal reforms that would aim at diminishing rape, increase rape convictions, and, overall, thoroughly protect Indian women from violence. The Verma Committee members were as follows: a former judge of the High Court, a former Solicitor General, and the committee head, Justice J.S. Verma, former Chief Justice of the Supreme Court (*Justice Verma Committee Report Summary*, 2015). Within a month, the committee released a comprehensive, 630-page report, which recommended reforms to the rape laws, sexual harassment laws, trafficking laws, and gender education in schools (*Justice Verma Committee Report Summary*, 2015).

Considering the recommendations of the Verma Report, the Indian government introduced the Criminal Law (Amendment) Bill in March, 2013, which was later signed by President Pranab Muherjee on April 2, 2013 (Drache & Velagic, 2014, p. 30). The bill included many of the committee's recommendations, including a broader redefinition of rape. According to the original Indian Penal Code of 1860, the definition of rape was limited to "penile penetration into the vagina" (Drache & Velagic, 2014, p. 30). Since the amendment, the definition of rape has been expanded to include penetration of the anus, vagina, or mouth, and penetration by a foreign object. The bill introduced police reforms, including a mandate to report all rapes and sexual assaults, and healthcare facilities are now required to provide free and immediate care to sexual assault or acid attack victims (Nundy, 2013).

However, the bill differed from the Verma report in a few, significant ways. First, the new amendment remained silent on the issue of marital rape. The Verma Committee, when arguing for its criminalization, disagreed with the notion that marriage establishes irrevocable consent between partners. However, because marriage is viewed as private within Indian culture, sacred and removed from government intervention, marital rape remained immune. In addition, contrary to recommendations, the Criminal Law (Amendment) Bill also introduced the possibility of the death penalty for rapes that result in death or a persistent vegetative state. The committee reasoned against the death penalty due to the strongly supported belief that it fails to deter serious crimes, including rape. Similarly, the committee recommended against the use of chemical castration, a recommendation which is currently being debated within the Indian Parliament. The committee argued that forced castration is unsuccessful because it "fails to treat the social foundations of rape which is about power and sexually deviant behaviour" (Verma, Seth, & Subramanium, 2013, p. 253).

The issue over the degrading and controversial two-finger test was also briefly explored in the Verma Committee report. According to the Verma Committee:

> It is crucial to underscore that the size of the vaginal introitus has no bearing on a

case of sexual assault, and therefore a test to ascertain the laxity of the vaginal muscles which is commonly referred to as the two-finger test must not be conducted. On the basis of this test observations/conclusions such as "habituated to sexual intercourse" should not be made and this is forbidden by law. (Verma, Seth, & Subramanium, 2013, p. 275)

Regardless of protest, the two-finger test remains a legal practice in India, leaving many women susceptible to re-victimization during the treatment and evidence gathering processes ("Degrading 'Test' for Rape," 2010).

While the Indian government has adopted numerous amendments in order to address systematic sexual violence against women, it has been largely unsuccessful at actually decreasing rates of sexual violence. Conviction rates for rapes in India remain extremely low. In 1974, the conviction rate was 39%, with 996 rape cases leading to convictions; comparatively, in 2011, only 26% of the reported rape cases ended in conviction of the perpetrator (Wright, 2013). The conviction rate continued to decrease, with only 24% of the 24,923 cases leading to convictions in 2012 (Bagchi, 2014). The success of the most recent reforms cannot be determined because the conviction rates have not been published by the NCRB. However, the number of reported rapes continues to increase, demonstrating the reforms' inability to reduce instances of sexual violence.

Police apathy is cited as a main institutional obstacle that rape victims face in seeking justice (Harris, 2013). Within major cities, a large portion of the police force is recruited from the neighboring rural areas. Consequently, these police officers retain their traditional, and oftentimes primitive views which inevitably result in victim blaming (Harris, 2013). As an example, in Haryana, a senior officer blamed the increase of rapes on easily persuaded girls and Western styled clothing (Denver, 2013). Additionally, many police officers prioritize the victim's honor over pleas of justice. Thus, to salvage a rape victim's tarnished honor, many police officers encourage victims to marry their rapist (Harris, 2013). Moreover, like many Indians, police officers frequently ignore violence between spouses, due to the private nature of

the crime. Consequently, many police officers do not file the appropriate paperwork needed to report the crime, further exacerbating the issue of underreporting (Human Rights Watch, 2009).

Panchayats, the unconstitutional tribal courts in rural areas of India, are viewed by many as their only source for justice. This is due to the inefficient workings of the Indian judiciary, namely the high costs associated with filing a formal complaint and the inaccessibility of formal courts to the countryside (Chaudhuri & Rajan, 2004). The existence of panchayats in rural India also limits the ability of Indian law to prosecute and convict rapists. Their deeply entrenched values of honor and male superiority disproportionately condemn women to cruel and unusual punishments. These punishments often include instances of sexual violence. This was demonstrated on January 21, 2014, when a young woman was sentenced to be gang raped by eleven men due to her illicit company with a Muslim man (Bagchi, 2014).

In the U.S. it is estimated that one in four women experience some form of physical or sexual abuse during their lifetime (The White House Council on Women and Girls & the Office of the Vice President, 2014). Additionally, in regards to sexual violence, 70% of all murders related to intimate partner violence are committed against women (The White House Council on Women and Girls & the Office of the Vice President, 2014). The U.S. is among the world's largest economies, and it is a predominantly caucasian, westernized society. Similar to India, the U.S. gained its independence from Britain. This fact suggests that the U.S.' government, culture, and laws were significantly influenced by the British, and sheds light on the concept of women as property. Chief Justice Sir Matthew Hale, a respected judge in Britain during the 1600s, was a major proponent of this idea. Accordingly, Hale delivered many judgements and cautions against supposed female rape victims. He espoused the notion that "rape is an accusation easily to be made, hard to be proved, and harder to be defended by the party accused, tho' never so innocent" (McGlynn & Munro, 2010). Concerning marriage, Hale decreed that wives could not be raped on account of their binding consent given in matrimony (Caringella, 2009).

In response to the growing number of rape cases in the U.S., a movement focused on women's rights began to form in the 1960s and 1970s, about a decade earlier than the movement in India. This social movement focused on rape prevention, legislative reform and victim support (Hodgson & Kelley, 2002). Prior to legislative reform, the anti-rape movement focused on the establishment of rape crisis centers that provide victim support along with d community education programs that primarily dealt with gender and sexuality. Additionally, similar to the reform movement in India, the legal code in the U.S. underwent significant reform. However, most of the reforms occurred at the state level and resulted in differentiation. In 1974, Michigan was the first state to adopt substantial changes to its penal code, motivated by the 56% increase of rapes in Michigan between 1969 and 1975 (Hodgson & Kelley, 2002). Consequently, many states based their laws on the Michigan model, which was arguably the most progressive (Caringella, 2009).

The reforms in Michigan were outlined in the Criminal Sexual Conduct Code, 1974, which introduced the model of graduation, and outlined varying degrees of criminal sexual conduct. Within the Michigan Penal Code, rape is categorized under four different degrees, including three felony categories and one misdemeanor category (Hodgson & Kelley, 2002). Additionally, the Michigan reforms prohibit the introduction of a victim's past sexual conduct, and this prohibition is often termed "shield laws" (Caringella, 2009). The inclusion of a victim's past sexual conduct was a tactic utilized by the defense with the intention of demonstrate the victim's promiscuity and, ultimately, fault for the sexual assault. However, after the introduction of this reform, the trial was mandated to focus solely on the specific assault in contention (Caringella, 2009).

Another reform included the removal of corroboration and resistance requirements. Historically, instances of sexual violence were the only serious crimes that dealt with legal corroboration requirements because of the prevalent rape myths claiming that women falsify rape reports. The criminalization of marital rape was also introduced in Michigan, in direct opposition to Hale's dated arguments. While marital rape was the most controversial reform, by 1993, all 50 states adopted this reform (Caringella,

2009). Additional reforms extended protection to previously unrepresented groups, such as male victims. These kinds of reforms were reflected in the use of sex-neutral terminology as it pertained to sexual crimes. Additionally, the biased requirement that victims take a polygraph test was removed. This reform confirmed the shift away from victim doubting by focusing instead on the motivations and actions of the defendant.

While the rape reforms of the 1970s and 1980s were successful in increasing victims' protections and legitimacy, they had little effect on the cultural perceptions of rape. In order to address this gap, President Clinton ratified the Violence against Women Act (VAWA) on September 13, 1994. This bill, originally introduced in 1990 by then-Senator Joe Biden, attempted to introduce legal and institutional changes concerning the prevention and response to sexual violence (Caringella, 2009). Included within the bill was a provision that automatically doubled sentences for repeat offenders in federal cases. Additionally, the shield laws that protect victims' past sexual histories were introduced into the federal jurisdiction. Infrastructural and institutional reforms included the ratification of VAWA, which authorized the distribution of large funds to increase public safety. These funds are continuously granted to various organizations, including the Department of Transportation in order to improve lighting, camera surveillance, and telecommunications. In addition, the allotted funds for institutional reforms were intended to improve enforcement of the rape laws. Under the auspices of the second chapter, large sums of money are granted to police agencies as a way of ensuring staff workers are developed, trained, and sensitized appropriately (Caringella, 2009).

After the rape reforms were introduced, many studies were conducted to measure their effectiveness in protecting the victim and in punishing the perpetrator. While the results are varied, it is clear that the reforms were mainly unsuccessful (Caringella, 2009). Numerous studies, regarding corroboration requirements, have shown that while corroboratory evidence requirements are *de jure* prohibited, they are still *de facto* required for prosecutors to try the case and for juries to convict. This idea was echoed by an Atlanta lawyer: "'You still win or lose on your corroboration'" (as cited in Caringella, 2009, p. 30).

Various studies demonstrate that shield laws are often ignored by both officials and lawyers during trial, especially in cases where the victim has admitted to previous sexual contact with the defendant. Spohn and Horney's (1992) investigation found that of the numerous officials they interviewed, most agreed that previous sexual encounters have a 50% chance of being introduced as evidence (Caringella, 2009). Numerous studies also prove that conviction rates have not increased due to legislative reform, although there has been a slight increase in arrest rates (Caringella, 2009). However, these same studies concluded that the rate at which police officers declared rapes unfounded remained the same (Caringella, 2009).

Many researchers argue that these mixed results stem from the excessive discretion allowed to the executive and judicial branches. Police officers are afforded personal discretion to decide whether a criminal claim is founded or unfounded. Prosecutors are also afforded similar discretion, granting them the authority to decide whether or not to try cases in court. This discretion becomes problematic when police officers and prosecutors internalize the various patriarchal rape myths which can produce bias against the victim (Caringella, 2009). One of the most frequently cited rape myths used to excuse or minimize rape is the notion that women who experienced sexual violence were "asking for it," due to their provocative clothing or behavior (Shaw & Lee, 2008). Many others claim that feminists exaggerate the actual number of rapes that occur; this notion is often accompanied by the belief that women frequently falsify rape reports. According to this belief, women tend to falsely accuse men in order to preserve their reputation or to take revenge. However, according to statistics collected by the Federal Bureau of Investigation, only 3% of rape allegations are false, matching the rates of other serious crimes (Levit & Verchick, 2006).

The failures of the legal reforms in both India and the U.S. demonstrate the law's limited ability to enact social change. While progressive laws have the potential to serve as models, they are ineffective without executive and judicial support. Accordingly, in order for laws to serve their intended purpose, the U.S. and Indian governments must increase the accountability of police officers and judicial officials. In addition, in order to facilitate social change, governments should incorporate gender issues into mainstream education. If taught about gender issues at young ages, girls would realize their potential and recognize their worth, and boys would learn to view their female classmates as equals (Winthrop, 2013).

Supporting social grassroots movements is another way in which governments can promote progressive, cultural change. Currently, the campaign "#VogueEmpower" is attempting to promote awareness of gender inequality in India. This campaign has gained a lot of media attention as it features famous celebrities in short films which revolve around gender issues. One of their films, "#StartWithTheBoys," depicts the negative social consequences of boys suppressing their emotions and advocates for the redefinition of gender roles (Thacker, 2015). Take Back the Night, an international advocacy movement, has become especially prevalent on college campuses; it encompasses events, vigils and marches designed to bring awareness to victims of sexual assault and rape. *Priya's Shakti*, a comic book that features a crime-fighting, tiger-riding woman, is another creative and successful social movement that advocates for the elimination of sexual violence. This comic, created by Ram Devineni, depicts a strong, courageous rape victim who works tirelessly to defend others from rape (Chatterjee, 2014). Governments can provide funds to promote the expansion of these organizations and endeavors. Governments can also create their own campaigns, which can potentially resemble the recent U.S. campaign, "It's On Us." This movement, recently announced by President Obama, encourages everyone to sign a pledge that vows to work towards ending sexual assault on college campuses (Somanader, 2014).

Both India and the U.S. have demonstrated their desire to decrease rates of sexual violence, and promote gender equality by enacting legislative changes. However, it is clear that legislation can be inhibited by the entrenched cultural norms of a society. Thus, while reforming laws constitutes as the first, necessary step to ending rape and sexual violence, a broader, more progressive shift must occur in societal gender norms, beliefs, and ideas in order to completely eradicate sexual violence.

REFERENCES

109A U.S.C. § 2241 (2013).

Annavarapu, S. (2013). Hetero-normativity and rape: Mapping the construction of gender and sexuality in the rape legislations in India. *The International Journal of Criminal Justice Science, 8*(2), 248-264.

Bagchi, I. (2014). The struggle for women's empowerment in India. *Current History, 113*(762), 144-146, 148-149.

Bagri, N. T. (2013). Where is India's feminist movement headed? *The New York Times.* Retrieved from http://nyti.ms/1ggr0TJ

Bhowmick, N. (2013, November 8). Why rape seems worse in India than everywhere else (but actually isn't). *Time.* Retrieved from http://ti.me/HKE9Ik

Bialik, C. (2013, August 31). Statistics shine little light on rape rates. *The Wall Street Journal.* Retrieved from http://on.wsj.com/17tytNr

Bridges, A. J., Wosnitzer, R., Scharrer, E., Sun, C., & Liberman, R. (2010). Aggression and sexual behavior in best-selling pornography videos: A content analysis update. *Violence Against Women, 16*(10), 1065-1085. doi:10.1177/1077801210382866

Burke, J. (2013, September 10). Delhi rape: How India's other half lives. *The Guardian.* Retrieved from http://gu.com/p/3g3ba/stw

Calman, L. J. (1989). Women and movement politics in India. *Asian Survey, 29*(10), 940-958.

Caringella, S. (2009). *Addressing rape reform in law and practice.* New York, NY: Columbia University Press.

Chatterjee, R. (2014, December 16). India's new comic book hero fights rape, rides on the back of a tiger. *NPR.* Retrieved from http://n.pr/1ACxbKt

Chaudhuri, M., & Rajan, R. S. (Eds.). (2004). *Feminism in India.* New York, NY: Zed Books Ltd.

Central Intelligence Agency. (2015a). India. In *The World Factbook.* Retrieved from https://www.cia.gov/library/publications/the-world-factbook/geos/in.html

Central Intelligence Agency. (2015b). United States. In *The World Factbook.* Retrieved from https://www.cia.gov/library/publications/the-world-factbook/geos/us.html

Das, S., Jain-Chandra, S., Kochhar, K., & Kumar, N. (2015). *Women workers in India: Why so few among so many?* (Working Paper No., 15/55). Tokyo, Japan: International Monetary Fund, Asia and Pacific Department. Retrieved from https://www.imf.org/external/pubs/ft/wp/2015/wp1555.pdf

Dasgupta, K. (2014, December 10). How can India end this tide of violence against women? *The Guardian.* Retrieved from http://gu.com/p/442xj/stw

Degrading "test" for rape, India. (2010). *Reproductive Health Matters, 18*(36), 226.

Delhi gang-rape victim dies in hospital in Singapore. (2012, December 29). *BBC News.* Retrieved from http://www.bbc.com/news/world-asia-india-20860569

Denyer, S. (2013, January 8). In rural India, rapes are common, but justice for victims is not. *The Washington Post.* Retrieved from https://www.washingtonpost.com/world/asia_pacific/in-rural-india-rapes-are-common-but-justice-for-victims-is-not/2013/01/08/c13546b4-58d6-11e2-88d0-c4cf65c3ad15_story.html

Department of Economic and Social Affairs. (2010). *The world's women 2010: Trends and statistics.* Retrieved from http://unstats.un.org/unsd/demographic/products/worldswomen/WW_full%20report_BW.pdf

Drache, D., & Velagic, J. (2014). Sexual violence journalism in four leading English language Indian publications before and after the Delhi rape. *Journal of Research in Gender Studies, 4*(2), 11-38.

Dutta, D., & Sircar, O. (2013). India's winter of discontent: Some feminist dilemmas in the wake of a rape. *Feminist Studies, 39*(1), 293-306.

Fed up with additional dowry demands, woman drowns daughters, self. (2014, December 5). *The Times of India.* Retrieved from http://toi.in/WhQRSY

Gangoli, G. (2007). *Indian feminisms: Law, patriarchies and violence in India.* Burlington, VT: Ashgate Publishing Company.

Gaynair, G. (2011, November 1). ICRW survey reveals contradictions in Indian men's views on gender equality. *International Center for Research on Women.* Retrieved from http://www.icrw.org/media/news/gender-equality-indian-mens-attitudes-complex

Guha, P., Kara, M., Shyam, S., Dogra, N., Mahajan, V., Dube, L., … Mazumdar, V. (1974). *Towards equality: Report on the committee on the status of women in India.* New Delhi, India: Government on India, Ministry of Education & Social Welfare.

Harris, G. (2013, January 12). For rape victims in India, police are often part of the problem. *The New York Times.* Retrieved from http://nyti.ms/ViOJeW

Hodgson, J. F., & Kelley, D. S. (Eds.). (2002). *Sexual violence: Policies, practices, and challenges in the United States and Canada.* Westport, CT: Greenwood Publishing Group.

Human Rights Watch. (2009, August 4). *Broken system: Dysfunction, abuse, and impunity in the Indian police.* Retrieved from https://shar.es/1YLI9K

Inter-Parliamentary Union. (2015, February 1). *Women in national parliaments* [Data set]. Retrieved from http://www.ipu.org/wmn-e/world.htm

Jain, J. (2011). *Indigenous roots of feminism: Culture, subjectivity and agency.* Thousand Oaks, CA: SAGE Publications.

Justice Verma committee report summary. (n.d.). Retrieved from http://www.prsindia.org/parliamenttrack/report-summaries/justice-verma-committee-report-summary-2628/

Katzenstein, M. F. (1989). Organizing against violence: Strategies of the Indian women's movement. *Pacific Affairs, 62*(1), 53-71.

Kolaskar, A. S., & Dash, M. (2012). *Women and society: The road to change.* New Delhi, India: Oxford University Press.

Koss, M. P. (1993). Rape: Scope, impact, interventions, and public policy responses. *American Psychologist, 48*(10), 1062-1069. doi:10.1037/0003-066X.48.10.1062

Kristof, N., & WuDunn, S. (2009). *Half the sky: Turning oppression into opportunity for women worldwide.* New York, NY: Alfred A. Knopf.

Lama, P. (2014). Women empowerment in India: Issues and challenges. *International Journal of Multidisciplinary Approach & Studies, 1*(6), 387-399.

Lauzen, M. M., & Dozier, D. M. (2005). Maintaining the double standard: Portrayals of age and gender in popular films. *Sex Roles, 52*(7/8), 437-446. doi:10.1007/s11199-005-3710-1

Levit, N., & Verchick, R. R. M. (2006). *Feminist legal theory: A primer.* New York, NY: New York University Press.

London School of Hygiene & Tropical Health. (2013, June 20). Violence against women a global health problem of epidemic proportions. *London School of Hygiene & Tropical Medicine.* Retrieved from http://www.lshtm.ac.uk/newsevents/news/2013/gender_violence_report.html

McGlynn, C., & Munro, V. E. (Eds.). (2010). *Rethinking rape law: International and comparative perspectives.* New York, NY: Glasshouse.

National Science Foundation. (2013). *Demographic characteristics of employed scientists and Engineers, by sex: 2013* [Data file]. Retrieved from http://www.nsf.gov/statistics/2015/nsf15311/tables/pdf/tab9-38.pdf

Nundy, K. (2013, March 28). Explaining India's new anti-rape laws. *BBC News*. Retrieved from http://www.bbc.com/news/world-asia-india-21950197

Odem, M. E., & Clay-Warner, J. (Eds.). (1998). *Confronting rape and sexual assault*. Lanham, MD: SR Books.

Padmaja, S. (2008, May 26). Women take the lead in rural BPOs. *The Times of India*. Retrieved from http://toi.in/ZclS4a

Phadke, S., Ranade, S., & Khan, S. (2013). Invisible women. *Index on Censorship, 42*(40), 40-45. doi:10.1177/0306422013500738

Popovic, M. (2011). Pornography use and closeness with others in men. *Archives of Sexual Behavior, 40*(2), 449-456. doi:10.1007/s10508-010-9648-6

Renu A. (2014). Discursive and institutional intersections: Women, health and law in modern India. *International Review of Sociology, 24*(3), 488-502. doi:10.1080/03906701.2014.954327

Roberts, Y. (2015, February 28). India's daughter: 'I made a film on rape in India. Men's brutal attitudes truly shocked me'. *The Guardian*. Retrieved from http://gu.com/p/467qn/stw

Roy, S. (2014). New activist subjects: The changing feminist field of Kolkata, India. *Feminist Studies, 40*(3), 628-656, 725-726.

Roychowdhury, P. (2013). "The Delhi gang rape": The making of international causes. *Feminist Studies, 39*(1), 282-292.

S. 375, The Indian Penal Code, 1860.

Savage, C. (2012, January 6). U.S. to expand its definition of rape in statistics. *The New York Times*. Retrieved from http://nyti.ms/25K1WOZ

Sen, A. (2013, October 10). India's women: The mixed truth. *The New York Review of Books*. Retrieved from http://www.nybooks.com/articles/2013/10/10/indias-women-mixed-truth/

Sharma, R.R., Pardasani, R., & Nandram, S. (2014). The problem of rape in India: A multi-dimensional analysis. *International Journal of Managing Projects in Business, 7*(3), 362-379. doi:10.1108/IJMPB-10-2013-0061

Shaw, S. M., & Lee, J. (Eds.). (2008). *Women's voices, feminist visions: Classic and contemporary readings* (4th ed.). Mountain View, CA: McGraw-Hill Higher Education.

Sinha, K. (2014, April 7). British court slams Indian judiciary's slow pace. *The Times of India*. Retrieved from http://toi.in/79KDqa

Sirnate, V. (2014, February 1). Good laws, bad implementation. *The Hindu*. Retrieved from http://www.thehindu.com/opinion/lead/article5639799.ece

Smith, S., & Cook, C. A. (2008). Gender stereotypes: An analysis of popular films and TV. *The Geena Davis Institute on Gender in Media*. Retrieved from http://annenberg.usc.edu/pages/~/media/MDSCI/Gender%20Stereotypes.ashx

Somanader, T. (2014, September 19). President Obama launches the "It's On Us" campaign to end sexual assault on campus. *The White House*. Retrieved from http://whitehouse.gov/blog/2014/09/19/president-obama-launches-its-us-campaign-end-sexual-assault-campus

Subramaniam, M. (2004). The Indian women's movement. *Contemporary Sociology, 33*(6), 635-639.

Thacker, P. (2015, March 29). Indian women come together to deliver a powerful message of empowerment and choice. *The New York Times*. Retrieved from http://nytlive.nytimes.com/womenintheworld/2015/03/29/indian-women-come-together-to-deliver-a-powerful-message-of-empowerment-and-choice/

The White House Council on Women and Girls & the Office of the Vice President. (2014). *Rape and sexual assault: A renewed call to action.* Retrieved from https://www.whitehouse.gov/sites/default/files/docs/sexual_assault_report_1-21-14.pdf

UNICEF. (2014, November). *Percentage of girls and women 15-49 years old who consider a husband to be justified in hitting or beating his wife for at least one of the specified reasons* [Data file]. Retrieved from http://data.unicef.org/child-protection/attitudes.html

Valenti, J. (2014). *Full frontal feminism: A young woman's guide to why feminism matters.* Berkeley, CA: Seal Press.

Verma, J. S., Seth, L., & Subramanium, G. (2013). *Report of the committee on amendments to criminal law.* Retrieved from http://www.thehindu.com/multimedia/archive/01340/Justice_Verma_Comm_1340438a.pdf

Winthrop, R. (2013, January 15). Promoting gender equality through education in India. *Up Front.* Retrieved from http://www.brookings.edu/blogs/up-front/posts/2013/01/15-gender-equality-winthrop

Wright, T. (2013, January 9). A short history of Indian rape-law reforms. *The Wall Street Journal.* Retrieved from http://on.wsj.com/16dx751

Yardley, J. (2012, June 14). In Mumbai, a campaign against restroom injustice. *The New York Times.* Retrieved from http://nyti.ms/LNicYn

Yee, A. (2013). Reforms urged to tackle violence against women in India. *The Lancet, 381*(9876), 1445-1446. doi:10.1016/S0140-6736(13)60912-5

www.ingramcontent.com/pod-product-compliance
Lightning Source LLC
Chambersburg PA
CBHW081250040426
42452CB00015B/2774